the

lies

my

alcohol

told

me

for all of the women and men, trying to
hide pain & sadness behind their big,
drunken smiles.

contents

acknowledgements

Britney Leal & Jamye Fontillas for the incredible cover design

Anna Krusinski for polishing up my ramblings

& all the friends and family who have supported my alcohol free journey

introduction

I had never thought of myself as an author. Yet here I sit, writing my first
book. About myself. And my alcohol addiction. And all of the vulnerable
moments that came before, during, and after. Writing about myself
transports me directly back to middle school, with all those feelings of
awkwardness and discomfort. I like to think of people in two categories:
those who post about their experiences, encounters, and feelings on
Facebook and those who don't. If it isn't clear already, I fall into the latter
group. More specifically, I am the one who types out an entire post,
contemplates posting for about three minutes, and then deletes it all while
telling myself that it would be ridiculous to share that part of myself on
social media.

And yet here I am, writing a book about my life. It dawned on me while I was working one day (at home because I am writing this from quarantine) that it is bullshit for me to sit on all of the things I've learned about living my life and leveling up. A lot has changed in my life to lead to this exact moment when I am sitting in my leggings and oversized tee while sipping on freshly brewed coffee at 7 p.m. on a Wednesday.

My pivotal moment happened a few days (or maybe weeks?) after my wedding. I woke up trying to think of the special moments with Ian and it was all a blur. Yeah, yeah...everyone says you won't really remember your wedding day because it goes by so quickly. But that wasn't it. I had started my morning with mimosas and, as the morning progressed, I transitioned to just champagne. The night ended with wine and a burger from some restaurant that just happened to be open late. I know it was fun; my friends and family told me they enjoyed themselves. But in that moment when I couldn't recall memories from my own wedding day, I realized that I was allowing my life to slip past me. This was when I started to casually play with the idea of radically changing my life. I began wondering what my life would look like without alcohol. And I really liked how that looked.

This isn't just a story about my sober journey. It is about how I began to recognize that I was numbing myself to the life I was living. It is about my first ah-ha moment, the one when I finally woke up to see that I was no longer a recent college graduate. It was a life-changing, earth-shattering realization that completely shifted the trajectory of my life. It was then that I could finally see all of the lies that alcohol had been feeding me over the years. A fog was lifted, and for the first time in my adult life, I began to view the world around me with crystal clarity.

Because I typically need to be told something a thousand times before actually listening to the Universe (or God, or whatever you choose to believe), I needed one more jolt to finally drop the BS and step into my life. By this point, I had made it through two full years of sobriety. It was simultaneously the most difficult and rewarding thing I have ever done. Maybe people talk about this (and I've just been reading the wrong books and listening to the wrong podcasts), but no one ever told me that my decision to stop drinking would essentially wipe the slate clean. I was starting over. I had spent the past eight-ish years revolving around the next party, that after-work drink, any way I could numb myself from my reality with alcohol. I had no idea who I was. I had no idea what I liked. And I realized that I was going to have to relearn everything about myself in order to stick to my new sober life.

Prior to my decision to stop drinking, I had a very specific vision of what an "alcoholic" looked like, and it wasn't me. I had begun to believe that alcohol was the only way to have fun or feel confident. I laughed off my blackouts like they were a totally normal part of life. I was truly convinced that my mental health was great and that my life had been nothing short of peachy. Sobriety, on the other hand, allowed me to break free from those lies, and it plunged me directly in the middle of a healing journey that I sure as hell was not ready for.

That is part of the reason why I am writing this book. Everything came as a complete shock to me when I first stopped drinking. And by shock I truly mean that I was far from prepared for the journey ahead of me. I believed sobriety was a simple decision to stop drinking. I didn't consider how it would totally change the fabric of my life. I learned—through each of the highs and every single fucking low—that sobriety was about choosing again, choosing to live life as my actual authentic self rather than the sad lonely person I had been embodying during my drinking years.

Sobriety is an opportunity to change your mind and decide that you will no longer settle for the clouded vision, the avoidance, and the lies. Sobriety is a superpower that I had been unable to see until I gave it a go.

It is safe to say that the first two years of my sobriety were a daily struggle to stay sober. I removed myself from the party scene. I lost a few friends who couldn't support my decision. And I picked up all of the hobbies. I explored different jobs, I read new books, and I tried new things. Now, I can't remember the exact date when it happened, but I woke up one morning in December, just a few months after my second sober anniversary, with a realization that literally shook me to my core. The one thought pounding in my head was, *What the fuck have you been doing?*

In that moment, I reviewed my life thus far. Sure, I had gone to college, and I now have a job with health benefits. But what had I actually done with my life over the past twenty-eight years? I know at one point I had goals and dreams, but those seemed like a part of my distant past. I wondered when I had stopped working toward my goals, when I had told myself that my dreams were unrealistic, when I had decided to float along in life as a passive observer rather than an active participant. I was proud of myself for my two years of sobriety and the various hobbies I had picked up along the way but I knew I had more work to do.

You know that feeling you get first thing in the morning before your body is fully awake? Your eyes feel fuzzy, your head is groggy. I felt like I was emerging from one of those moments, but with my *life*. I was finally waking up after years and years of passive sleep. As I looked back at my life, I saw where I had avoided the feelings, the struggles, and the anxieties. And in doing so I had numbed myself to the life I was living. I had let go of my dreams. I had forgotten about the woman I once desired to become when I was younger.

So on this seemingly unremarkable December morning, it all came flooding back—the goals, and the dreams, and the aspirations. I was able to see the version of myself that I had been striving to become before I had lost my way. During this literal flood of thoughts and emotions, I saw a long-forgotten book sitting on my bedside table. I had purchased it based on a friend's recommendation (hey, Ashley!), but had decided that personal development books weren't for me. That day was different, though. That day, I threw out all of my old ideas about basically everything. In what I now see as a fit of glory, I picked up *You Are a Badass* by Jen Sincero and finished reading it in the better part of a day.

Reading Jen's book felt like a very loud alarm going off in my head. And I needed more. I needed to read more about women who were shredding the rule books and stepping into their truths. I needed to surround myself with inspirational and motivational women who were unapologetically living their best lives. So that's what I did. In fact, I deleted my Instagram to start over fresh; to fill my immediate (social media) reality with fucking motivated, inspirational, gorgeous women. I signed up for every free class and webinar I could find. I binge-listened to podcast interviews. I tore through so many more books.

I went from being someone who had avoided personal development like the plague to someone who literally could not get enough. Somewhere in that whirlwind of reading, listening, and absorbing things started to click. Those phrases I had heard offhand years ago actually made sense now. The realities these incredible women have crafted for themselves didn't feel like some elusive dream anymore. I finally understood. *I am the creator of my own reality.* I've always had the keys to my kingdom. I just needed to wake up to know they were there.

That brings us to this moment as I am furiously typing away on my laptop while listening to the gentle patter of rain outside my house. While I was rediscovering myself, I felt continually drawn to share my story, my realizations, my epiphanies. And I've finally decided to do it. If it weren't for others who have shared their stories with the world, I wouldn't be where I am today. We are not alone on this planet. We are not supposed to do this thing called "life" without any support. We are here to lift each other up, cheer each other on, and continue to level up together. Knowing all of this, I figure it would be rude for me to hide my story from the world because if only one person reads this book and finds meaning in its pages, it will have served its purpose.

And here we are. At the end of the introduction to my book about my life and all of the lies my alcohol told me.

—*Natasha Mason, August 2020*

my first

I started drinking when I was seventeen years old. By that time, I had
made it through most of my high school experience without alcohol.
Why? Honestly, I had been so focused on myself and my goals that I
didn't even have time to consider drinking. I was throwing all of my energy
into school and swimming. I had this dream that I would swim at a Big
Ten school and make it to the Olympic Trials. I was going to graduate
college with some great degree and do something truly significant with my
life.

When I was younger, I had this unabashed confidence. I truly believed
that I could do absolutely anything, and that included swimming. I loved
to swim. The quiet and the calm of the water was my safe place. The daily
challenge of pushing myself to be better was exhilarating. I absolutely

loved jumping into the pool each day for practice, and I looked forward to every single meet. I was obsessed. So I set my sights on the highest possible goal in the sport: the Olympics.

But over the years things stopped being so easy. I started to find that I couldn't make it through an event at a swim meet without having a panic attack. It was as if my love for swimming was becoming overshadowed by the pressure I was putting on myself to constantly improve, to always be better. I stopped dropping time. And I started to question my goals and my dreams. I began to wonder if I was even meant to continue swimming.

In this space, as I was shifting my focus away from swimming, I began to consider things that had previously never crossed my mind. I wondered if maybe I had been missing out by not going to parties. I thought that smoking weed could actually be fun. I even grew bored with the thought of solely focusing on my studies.

At that point, I decided to give drinking a try.

Once I did, I did not let it go. My first time drinking was at my friend's house. Her parents were home, but they didn't care if we were drinking as long as we stayed in the house. So we pulled out bottles of liquor and just started taking shots. I remember feeling light, giggly, free. As we danced through the kitchen and twirled each other around, I felt at ease. While I was drunk, I didn't have to think about arguing with my mom or about the tests I would take the following week. While I was drunk, I wasn't worried about whether I would have a date to prom. Alcohol seemed like this beautiful liquid gold that allowed me to just let go and enjoy the present moment.

While I was drunk, I stopped stressing about getting perfect grades. I stopped worrying about what college I would go to or whether there would be enough scholarship money to pay the tuition. I no longer felt like I had somehow failed my high school experience by not having a boyfriend or even a guaranteed date to prom. The panic attacks I was having during swim meets and at night, alone in my room, no longer felt so serious. And best of all, while I was drunk, I could simply ignore any emotions other than feeling happy. I didn't have to acknowledge my fears of the future. Or the sadness I felt about my dad living across the country during my senior year. And especially the feelings of darkness and hopelessness that seemed to pop up at random despite this "perfect" and "happy" life I was leading.

That was the first lie alcohol told me: as long as I was drinking, the pain, and sadness, and fear would all fade away.

peppermint schnapps

Looking back over my drinking years, it is easy to see how my relationship with alcohol was far from healthy. And I'm talking about from day one. That first sip took me out of my body and away from my emotions. It wrapped me in a suffocating blanket that isolated me from the world. I continued to chase that sweet relief of escapism for the rest of my drinking years.

There was never a point in time when I had healthy drinking habits. The first time I drank, we took shots until we were drunk. The second, third, fourth, and twentieth time was some variation of that first time. Enter: college. As I was living on my own, surrounded by other people who were drinking every night of the week—people who encouraged me to drink and party because it was the thing to do—my drinking began to spiral. After graduation, I became a more sophisticated drinker by selecting nicer wines and bottles of gin. But at no point during those years did I have a handle on my drinking. After that first night, I was slowly spinning out of control.

•••

There is this one story that I've effectively avoided talking about since the day it happened. Part of me knew it was unhealthy while it was happening but I was able to convince myself that it was actually fine. One night, when I was still in high school, I had planned to go to a friend's house to drink but something fell through. Rather than let that put a damper on my night, I took a bottle of peppermint schnapps from my parent's liquor cabinet, settled down on the couch in the basement, and drank by myself.

First, peppermint schnapps? An absolutely terrible choice. And I am honestly grateful it didn't ruin my love of mint-flavored everything. Second, I was drinking alone. I was drinking alone in my parent's basement while I was still in high school.

I don't need to go into more detail about why this was so unhealthy. But this was the first time that I began to normalize drinking alone. I was drunk and I felt good. That was all that mattered to me in the moment. Afterward, I simply chose not to think about it. There was absolutely a part of me that knew it was not okay to get drunk alone. But that's the thing with alcohol; you become really fucking good at simply avoiding the difficult thoughts, the ones that would challenge the shiny new lies alcohol is feeding you.

And it taught me how to lie. There is nothing like hearing your mother come down into the basement to check on you while you are super drunk—alone—to teach you how to get your shit together enough for her not to notice. Looking back, I'm sure she was concerned to find her teenage daughter sitting alone in the basement and watching a movie in the dark, especially when Friday nights were typically spent with my parents and siblings playing a board game, watching a movie, or simply hanging out.

So, when I heard my mom's footsteps on the basement stairs, I quickly hid the bottle and allowed my body to relax into the chair, and into the bullshit I was about to speak into existence. I remember speaking with precision, enunciating every syllable in order to avoid sounding even the least bit inebriated. Looking back, I'm certain that I was able to effectively hide this from my mom because she hadn't been expecting it. She never could have imagined I had been drinking. It was something so drastically different from what I had been doing the previous three years of high school, so of course the thought wouldn't have even crossed her mind.

The next day, I didn't feel guilty about lying and hiding my night of solo drinking. I reframed the situation as an act of rebellion on my part. I was choosing to break away from the strict lifestyle in which my parents had raised me. I allowed the thrill of drinking—and hiding it from my mom—to sweep me away into this idea that I was beginning to live life on my terms, not as my parents wanted me to.

My alcohol told me that lying to hide my drinking was an acceptable way to live.

$\bullet\bullet\bullet$

I've never told anyone that story. Apparently, I was waiting to write a book about my tumultuous history with alcohol before sharing this little gem. Recalling this experience used to cause me physical pain, as though something had a vice grip on my stomach. It was too embarrassing to share. And it would have required me to acknowledge that my drinking was always out of control, that I was chasing that drunk feeling from the very beginning.

Now when I think of that memory, my heart breaks for that girl. The girl who wanted to escape and avoid so desperately that she justified drinking alone at seventeen.

All of this goes to say, don't take fucking shots of peppermint schnapps in your parent's basement, especially if you are *alone*. And don't assume that someone isn't struggling just because they seem okay on the surface. There is documented proof that even the kids who seem to have it together—the ones who have straight A's, play on a varsity sports team, and are getting a massive scholarship to a private university—may be struggling.

At some point, I began to allow myself to heal from that experience. The healing wasn't instant; it was a process that required me to dismantle all of the untruths I had convinced myself of. But for the longest time, I sure as hell did not think this was an experience I needed to heal from, especially in my early drinking years. I had honestly told myself so many times that "everyone did this" until I began to believe that it was true. And my college experience did nothing to dispel the lie.

I'll say it again: healing is gradual. It takes time. I mean, that's what this book is, a form of healing. More than three years into sobriety, I am still releasing the shame, and the pain, and the embarrassment. I am choosing again. I am rewriting my story.

the in crowd

That first lie was the one that hooked me. I thought I had finally found a way to escape my own brain.

At some point in my childhood, I had told myself that I did not fit in, that I was not enough. I was convinced that my classmates did not want to be my friends. And certainly, there was no possibility that a boy could ever be interested in me. I told myself that I would always be on the outside looking in. This idea that I was not enough had permeated so much of my life in the way I acted, in the beliefs I held, and in the relationships I formed with other people.

This belief stemmed from the high standards that had been set for me and around me. I've always been a high achiever, even a perfectionist (although I now no longer proudly label myself as a perfectionist). And I embodied my parents' levels of education and their success in their careers. I had set my sights on the highest level of achievement in swimming I could imagine—going to the Olympics—because then my dad (the multiple all-American college wrestler) would see that I, too, had been exceptional in my sport of choice. I dreamed of getting straight A's and maintaining a perfect GPA, just like my mom had done when she was in school. I planned to attend Harvard or Yale because those schools were, in my mind, at the pinnacle of academic success.

At some point, I began to believe that achieving this high level of success was the only way I could earn my parents' love, attention, and pride. I soon began striving for perfection in order to be accepted by everyone—teachers, family, coaches. Plus, I felt like I was competing against everyone else around me including the kids I went to school with and my siblings.

That's the thing with fucked-up perceptions like this. "Enough" is never really enough. Despite all of my efforts and achievements, I only ever focused on my shortcomings, like the first B I got in my AP history class or the time I had a panic attack during states and didn't make it back to the finals.

But after that first night of taking shots with a few of my teammates in high school, that all started to change. Finally, I had something else to focus on. I had the validation of being in the "in" crowd. The next day, some of our other teammates were talking about the mini party we had had the night before. I was included in this group of girls who had shared in a fun night of drinking. That was the second lie alcohol told me. I believed that when I was drinking, I finally fit in. I was no longer on the outside wondering what it was like on the inside.

It felt amazing. I felt as though I had finally arrived, that I was finally living my life to the fullest and that I had finally found a way to break free from feeling like I was not enough. I fit in. I had friends. I was invited to parties. People wanted to hang out with me.

And that lie—that alcohol gave me a seat at the cool table—was reinforced time and time again. At our prom after-party, I was a part of the group of kids who were appropriately celebrating. And during the summer before I started college, I was invited to the parties. I even remember sneaking wine coolers at a graduation party and feeling so cool because I had dared to rebel.

Over and over, these superficial friendships and feelings of happiness gave me more and more reasons to buy into the lie. Until, at a certain point, it simply became an integral part of my life.

•••

My freshman year of college landed me in a dorm across campus from the rest of the freshmen. I was just a short walk from where the seniors on the swim team lived. On one of my first nights on campus, I was invited to their place to hang out. I showed up in my T-shirt, shorts, and fuzzy pink slippers ready to give that game of beer pong my all. I know for a fact that I looked ridiculous. But I didn't care because I knew that the minute I started drinking, I would fit in regardless of what I was wearing. And I did. I remember going to bed that night and thinking about how the seniors probably thought I was so much fun. I was the girl who could fit into any social situation with a beer in one hand and a shot in the other.

As time went on, alcohol continued to tell me new lies. It told me that it is easier to drink than it is to have a difficult conversation with a roommate.

It told me that it doesn't really matter what you do when you're drunk. And, in fact, the crazier the situation, the better the story the next day.

It convinced me that dating certain boys was a good idea.

And it introduced me to other substances that were just as effective at numbing as alcohol.

But the biggest lie of all was that my life was simply better with alcohol, and without it, I would be a nobody. Before I started drinking, I had felt alone. I never thought I was enough for anyone. And I always saw myself on the outside of the fun, the friendships, and of life in general. After that first drink, all those thoughts and feelings fell away, and I was left with the belief that alcohol could make my life more enjoyable.

the job of the party girl

We're supposed to take up space. Our voices are meant to be heard. Our lives are meant to be lived unapologetically. But somewhere along the way, I had internalized the messages I had been receiving from adults, teachers, friends, and the media. I began to believe that there was a specific way for me to show up in the world. That I can take up space but not too much. That I can speak up but not too loudly. And that I can live my life but I had to follow a set of specific guidelines. I was always painfully aware of other's expectations, which often came into conflict with one another. Depending on who you asked, I was expected to be fun. Or to be a lady. To not show *too much* emotion. Or to just be agreeable.

In the midst of all these expectations, I was stuck with the idea that I needed to dim my shine in order to fit in. So, rather than expressing my own unique version of myself, I fell into a role I thought others had come to expect of me: I became the party girl. You know the one: she is the life of the party. She has lots of friends. She is always happy. This role seemed ideal for me. It appeared to be the best way for me to be visible, to be seen in my own life without having to define what *I* truly wanted to be.

I'm not going to blame this entirely on societal standards, though. There was a part of me that was too scared to be my authentic self. I held on to the shame and embarrassment I had felt when I was called weird for loving to read. I remembered what it felt like to be called obnoxious for allowing my passionate, energetic self to come out. Or to be called bossy for being outspoken. I desperately wanted to be seen by the people around me but I was afraid to show up as *me*. So becoming the party girl was the easier option.

These same fears were what initially kept me from sobriety. There was a part of me that knew—long before my actual decision to get sober, the moment when I put the bottle down—that all I would be left with was myself. And at that point in time, I hated myself. I had been conditioned to believe that I was not the ideal. So I continued drinking because when I was drinking I could become whomever I wanted to be for the night.

I could have people I called friends.

I could smile in pictures.

I would be invited to parties.

I would feel seen by my peers.

But none of it was real. It was just a role I was playing so I didn't have to be myself. And, honestly, it was exhausting. The people I called my friends weren't really my friends. I may have been smiling in pictures but inside I felt tired and sad. I was invited to parties but not because of my personality or who I was. And while I did feel seen, it wasn't really *me* people were seeing.

To some extent, this was also the reason I was hesitant to recover loudly. Admitting to the world that I was sober felt like acknowledging that I had failed. That I wasn't the fun, carefree life of the party. That I was, in fact, an actual human with trauma, and struggle, and feelings.

Before that, being the party girl worked for a while. I was simply floating along, allowing life to happen to me. Until at some point, I began to realize that this role no longer served me. I was not proud of myself or the things I was doing. I knew I was not the role model I wanted to be for my younger sisters.

But the scary thing was that I had no idea who I was anymore. I had completely lost sight of myself and my vision for my life. I was constantly busy with work, or school, or social activities but I wasn't actually sure if I enjoyed any of the things I was doing.

I graduated from college with three undergraduate degrees and absolutely no idea what I was going to do with the rest of my life. My degrees were in subjects I had enjoyed learning about but that was the only direction I had in college. Rather than searching for the potential career that was calling my name, I had settled for a fun night at the bar and a handful of degrees in disciplines that kept me just interested enough to avoid utter boredom.

Somehow, in the moment, it seemed fine. I mean, I had to get a job doing something, right? And as long as my bills were paid and I had money to spend at the bar, life was good. So I started working as a nanny, then as a barista, then as a teacher at a swim school, then at Trader Joe's, then at Zingerman's. I never stayed in one place very long but that never worried me because I always had a job and could always manage to stay afloat.

After undergrad, I took classes at a local community college. I took a geography class, a writing class, and a math class. They were all over the place. So why did I bother? Couldn't tell ya. It just seemed like the thing I should be doing.

I spent my weekends in bars and clubs with people I didn't really know, listening to music I wasn't sure I liked. I was completely lost and I knew it. But the thing is, instead of taking a step back from the party culture, I just dove in even further.

Drinking more nights a week.

Taking party drugs when the drinking was no longer enough.

Popping pills because life had become too much during the day and I no longer wanted to wait until my evening glass of wine to escape. I was bored. Bored with my life and with the people in it. Any substance that could distract me from the boredom became an integral part of my day.

I spent time with people who wanted to party as much as I did. The alternative was to acknowledge that my life had become an empty shell of drinking, partying, and avoiding. I ignored all feelings of guilt, or embarrassment, or shame by continuing to push them farther and farther down, layering more alcohol and drugs on top of them. I became the queen of avoidance.

•••

The job of the party girl is not glamorous. It is fucking miserable. I was in a constant state of desperation. I was desperate to be liked. Desperate to be seen. Desperate to cover up my true self.

Thinking about this girl now breaks my heart. All I want to do is go back in time and show her that she is enough; that she has always been enough.

This part of my story isn't uncommon. I see so many other girls who are stuck in the same patterns that I had been cycling through just a few years ago. I see so many sad eyes hidden by a massive drunken smile.

Fuck being the party girl. Fuck being anything other than your authentic self. There is no better feeling than being your honest-to-God self.

I am loud.

My personality takes up so much space.

I can be irritatingly high-maintenance.

I listen to podcasts all day long.

I blast music and host a mini concert for my shampoo bottles when I'm in the shower.

I am passionate, and I work my ass off to allow that passion to shine through in everything I do.

I am weird, and silly, and excitable.

I prefer leggings and a giant sweater above all other outfit options. Fun, colorful, comfy socks are my favorite item of clothing, and I own far more than is considered reasonable under any circumstances. I will always wear glasses that are a bit too big for my face because I hate seeing frames in my line of sight.

Sometimes I smile and laugh because I feel so much joy that it just spills out. Other times, I wrap myself in a blanket and sit on my couch in the dark because the world is just a little too much that day.

Speaking my truth, feeling my feelings, and being myself can be so incredibly hard sometimes. But the hardest days of being my authentic self simply do not compare to how utterly miserable I was as the party girl.

when the party collides with family

It's St. Patrick's Day sometime between 2009 and 2013. (I honestly cannot remember the year because my college years have begun to melt into each other.) I am home from school on spring break so I'm staying with my parents and my three younger siblings. My mom drives me to downtown Ann Arbor to meet up with one of my friends for our St. Patty's Day celebration. (At least I had the foresight to not drive myself.) When I get to the house where my friend is staying, she greets me with a massive sip from a plastic bottle filled with some bottom-shelf vodka. That's where my day begins.

I don't really remember when or where it ended. I have hazy memories of going to other houses and bars, all while toting a drink. What I can remember more clearly is calling my mom later in the evening to ask if she

25

could pick me up. I'm not sure if the original plan was for me to go home or stay at my friend's place—like I normally did when I was out drinking—but my parents were out to dinner downtown anyway, so they swung by to pick me up.

I remember seeing their car parked on the side of the street before I ran across the street to greet them and get in the car. I remember being super drunk and super chatty. I thought I was being great fun. And I was so drunk that I believed my parents were having fun with me.

They weren't. I can remember my dad making a comment about me keeping my drunk hands off of his leftovers from dinner, and I'm pretty sure my mom said something about not throwing up in the car. In the moment, I had laughed them off. Because that's what St. Patty's Day is all about, right? Getting so wasted that your parents have to pick your drunk ass up. In hindsight, I can see that no one—including myself—was actually having fun.

And then we got home. I hung out with my siblings in the living room for a short amount of time before heading to my bedroom where I fell asleep, still fully clothed and with my makeup on. I was far too drunk to remember how my younger sisters reacted to my antics.

● ● ●

My two worlds had just collided. Until that point, I had been relatively successful at separating my party life from my family life. That's not to say that I didn't ever drink around my family but my energy level when I was sitting around the fireplace with my parents and siblings was different than when I was on the dance floor at a bar with my friends.

26

I didn't realize it at the time, of course. I just thought it was a hilariously fun evening (or day?) out. I thought it was the funniest thing that my parents picked me up after an entire day of partying to celebrate a holiday that has become known as a drinking holiday. My alcohol had me convinced that I was living my life to the absolute fullest.

•••

I was sitting in my little sister's bedroom the other day. She is now fourteen and halfway through her freshman year of high school. We were chatting about writing books. Mine, of course, is this one here. Hers is a fiction novel with more detail and character development than I thought was possible from a fourteen-year-old. As we were sitting there talking, it struck me how much my relationship with her has changed over the years.

When I was drinking, I was flaky and superficial. Our relationship was a reflection of that. The number of times I would initiate plans to go on a sister dinner date or go to the Hands-On Museum—or really any variety of activities—and then bail at the last minute was one of my biggest points of shame after I stopped drinking. One day, while I was home from college for the summer, I was about to make plans with my sister again. My dad stopped me and told me that I needed to stop making plans with her just to break them. We would have a dinner date and she would look forward to it for days just for me to casually bail at the last second, leaving her devastated. He was trying to protect her—from me.

Now, in my sobriety, our relationship has deepened. We talk about our mutual interests. We share different strategies to manage our anxiety. We watch movies and listen to podcasts about true crime together. Because I'm no longer clouded by alcohol, I can be my full self with her. I can be the big sister I've always wanted to be.

Back to that day in my sister's bedroom, my memories of that St. Patrick's Day binge flooded back. I used to think about that day fondly, like it was something to be proud of. My mind had been focused on the day while I was out drinking. In hindsight, I could now focus on the juxtaposition of my party life and my family life.

It's striking when your worlds overlap like that. In my mind, I had worked so hard to separate those two parts of my life because I still wanted people to think I had it together, that I wasn't a mess of a party girl who was slowly losing sight of herself.

But on that day, the lines began to blur. On that day, small cracks began to develop in my facade. I was no longer this person who went out drinking with her friends on the weekend like a normal college student. My family was beginning to see the extent to which I drank every night when I went out. It became harder to uphold the image of the girl who had it together. And that day was just the beginning.

•••

This is one of those moments, like that night with the bottle of peppermint schnapps, when I can clearly see that my relationship with alcohol was far from healthy or normal. Sitting where I am now, with more than three years of sobriety under my belt, I can see the striking difference between the two lives I was living. I can see how desperately I was struggling to maintain the image of myself as an intelligent young adult with a bright future ahead of her. I can see how hard I was trying to numb myself to the world so that I could breeze through life without a care in the world, and how hard I was working to avoid going any deeper than the paper-thin surface.

the big blur

On August 5, 2017, I married Ian. It was an overly planned, overly expensive day. Whenever I've talked about it over the years, my friends and family have told me that they remember it fondly. They've told me how beautiful the venue was, how delicious the food tasted, and how much fun they had.

We had spent months planning for the big day. We picked a gorgeous outdoor venue with a barn. We found a caterer who could set up a burger bar on-site. And when our wedding day finally arrived, it all seemed to fall into place. On the outside, everything appeared perfect. But below the surface, the lure of alcohol was brewing like a dark cloud that would obscure much of what I would be able to remember about our "perfect" wedding day.

●●●

The night before our wedding, I drank way too much with my maid of
honor. Ian had suggested that we not drink the night before so we could
be present (and not hungover) for the wedding day. I wanted to do that.
But I ended up getting so drunk that I overslept my alarm and arrived late
for hair and makeup. From there, the day was a haze of alcohol and pills.

We drank mimosas while we got ready.

Then I took some Adderall to help with my hangover.

Plus Valium to help with my nerves.

And finally, champagne to celebrate.

There was no time for food, and by the end of the night I was so fucking
hungry that one of my friends ran out to get me a burger and fries from a
local restaurant.

I smiled, I mingled, I danced. But the majority of the day is a blur. And
not the "it goes by so fast" sort of blur.

●●●

It took me about a year to order prints of our wedding photos because
every single time I thought of that amazingly beautiful day, I just felt so
much shame. I wasn't even present for my own wedding. I had numbed
myself so much with drinks and pills, and I couldn't even see what I was
missing out on in the moment.

Afterward, I rarely wanted to talk about it with my friends or family because it was too painful to remember how much I drank on the day I married Ian. Our wedding had become this memory that I was secretly ashamed of because of how detached I had been from the day. But whenever I talked to others about it, I still felt like I needed to pretend that it had been a perfectly magical event. So I put on a smile and kept the lie to myself.

• • •

Leading up to my wedding, I had believed that alcohol was an essential part of the reception. Not only would we need to have an open bar for our guests but we would also need our own alcohol in order to celebrate the occasion. This image of what a wedding was supposed to look like—and honestly my vision of celebrating—stemmed from years of watching movies and TV shows where people always celebrated with a glass of champagne, a cocktail, or a glass of wine. And my own actions during my drinking years supported that. I always celebrated with alcohol regardless of the occasion.

Alcohol had continued to reinforce the lie that I needed to drink in order to properly celebrate, in order to have the ideal wedding.

Maybe a week (maybe longer) after the wedding, I decided to stop drinking for the first time. I was nowhere near ready to acknowledge that I was an addict but I was ready to decide that not drinking would be a healthier option for my life.

Two months after that, I drank for the very last time.

●●●

It took me so much longer to have an honest conversation with Ian about this. Early in my sobriety, I wanted to hide from those memories. Even though I was no longer drinking or taking any sort of drug, I was still using avoidance to heal and to cope.

I didn't want to face my fears. I didn't want to address my traumas. I didn't want to do the hard work. Sure, my problem was alcohol, but deeper than that, my problem was avoidance. So even once I stopped drinking, I still continued to avoid, just without alcohol. I pretended that the emotions I felt weren't real. I opted to instead feed myself the same line I had heard over and over from numerous adults in my life: that I was simply being overly sensitive. I skipped out on therapy the minute we began to dig deeper than the superficial anxieties I was willing to share. And now that I was sober, I realized that when I pushed deeper every feeling and thought seemed so much harder to face without alcohol. I tried not to fall into my old avoidance trap. And at some point, it became clear that the only way I was going to be able to move forward with my life was by addressing my past, by feeling my feelings, and by speaking my truth.

Once I finally decided to talk to Ian about our wedding day—to have the conversation I had convinced myself was going to be so terrible, and painful, and damaging—I was finally able to heal. I spoke out loud the thing I had feared, and the minute the light hit it, dragging it out of the shadows, it no longer had hold over me. It was no longer a secret that I was holding deep inside my soul, ashamed to admit to anyone, including the man I had chosen as my partner for life.

There are times when I'm feeling low and certain memories from that day will still make me cringe but now I can think about our wedding without feeling sick to my stomach. I have some photos hanging in our house; the others I just haven't gotten around to buying a frame for yet. I can finally reminisce about that day without feeling an overwhelming rush of guilt as though the entire thing had been a lie. I can now live in the truth of what that day was—and wasn't—and I can recognize it as a turning point in what would become my path to sobriety.

Being honest and vulnerable isn't easy. I don't think anyone has ever claimed it is easy. But the only way to grow is to allow yourself to heal from your past mistakes. And you sure as hell cannot heal from your past mistakes if you cannot speak honestly about them.

It started with our wedding, then I begrudgingly opened up about everything: the night I got drunk alone in my parent's basement, the toxic and emotionally abusive college boyfriend, the blackouts, and most importantly, my decision to embrace sobriety.

I laid myself and my mistakes out in front of me. As difficult as it was, I found that I still loved myself and I was proud of myself afterward.

addict

Addict.

Alcoholic.

Substance abuse.

Sober.

Alcohol-free.

These terms are common labels that we use to place people into convenient boxes, to attempt to tell someone's story with just a word or two. But when we think about the images that come to mind when we hear these labels, how often does the truth actually fit the stereotype?

Early in my sobriety, I struggled with how to define myself. Was I really an alcoholic? Was I a substance abuser? Could I now truly call myself sober? As I plunged myself into the deep end of removing alcohol from my life, these questions swirled in my mind, clouded by what I thought an alcoholic looked like.

●●●

Shortly after I decided to stop drinking, I was standing in my mother's kitchen as she was pulling things out of the fridge to make dinner. I was leaning against the counter when I blurted out, "Mom, I am an alcoholic," before launching into a longer explanation and finishing with, "But I am done drinking now."

My mom looked at me and said something along the lines of, "Well, you do drink a lot but do you really think you are an alcoholic?"

That is part of the problem. As I was growing up, I had imagined an alcoholic as a middle-aged white man. I thought alcoholism was something that only affected real adults, the ones who were in their forties, the ones who had actually lived a bit of their life.

That certainly couldn't have applied to me. Drinking in high school was acceptable. Partying in college was the norm. Drinks at brunch. Drinks at dinner. Drinks to celebrate. Drinks after a long day. Drinks just because. Drinking alone had been normalized. Blacking out had been glorified.

We are completely saturated in drinking culture to the point where excessive drinking is brushed over and true addictions are mislabeled. And so when my mom questioned the word I had used to describe myself, it did not come as a surprise. Nor did the questions and comments made by my friends and family throughout my sobriety.

I'm not telling you this story about my mom because of anything she did wrong. I don't blame my mom for not seeing my problem for what it truly was. Don't they always say that the last people to notice an addiction are those closest to the person suffering? Plus, who really thinks of a twenty-six-year-old recent college graduate as an alcoholic? Actually, my choice to stop drinking—to be sober and to stay sober—is a testament to how incredible my mom truly is, how incredible both my parents are. They are both strong and determined people, and they instilled that in me. So when I made the decision to stop drinking for good, and I acknowledged that my drinking was problematic, that was it. That was the last time I drank. That strength, and courage, and tenacity are qualities I learned from them. And their pride warms my heart and makes me smile.

I'm sharing this particular story because we have been coached by society on what we should think an alcoholic looks like. We have been trained to believe that a twenty-something kid could never be an addict. In fact, the concept of partying has been so normalized that it has been integrated into the very process of growing up. Kids will drink, right? Kids will party in college, right? They'll settle down eventually. It's just a phase; it won't last. But when does it stop being a phase and start becoming a problem?

The mere word "alcoholic" is deeply rooted in negative imagery. I would even go as far as to say that the word itself has become taboo. You don't want to mention your alcoholism to your colleagues, your boss, or anyone you interact with in a professional setting. The amount of disdain given to that one little word is astounding.

• • •

A few years later, I was sitting in my therapist's office telling her about a dinner I had planned with two of my work friends for the following Tuesday. I was excited to have the plans (especially because they involved tacos) but I was worried about how I would address the fact that I was not drinking. Actually, both of my friends already knew I didn't drink anymore but they didn't know *why*. I had built up this idea in my mind that the minute we sat down for dinner, they would order drinks and then ask me why I had stopped drinking.

I am already an anxious person (hence the therapist) but my fears in that moment were compounded. First, I knew I would be in a social situation where other people would be drinking. Although I had over two years of sobriety under my belt by that time, there was still the "what if" thoughts bouncing around in my brain. *What if I sit down at the table and all my sober resolve goes out the window? What if, in the midst of the fun, I say, "Fuck it," and decide to begin drinking again?*

Second, the two ladies I was going to dinner with were my coworkers, and the last thing I wanted to do was start sharing my history with alcohol. I was still holding my "alcoholic" card close to the chest. Only my close friends and immediate family knew. I was not ready to bare my deepest shame with the rest of the world.

Sitting there in my therapist's office, we worked through a few responses I could use if any of my "what if" situations were to arise. And then we practiced them until I landed on the response I felt most comfortable with: "I just decided I didn't want to drink anymore."

Lo and behold, our dinner date came, and while everyone was ordering margaritas and I ordered a lemonade, one of the women jokingly said, "So do you not drink because you're an alcoholic or something?" She had a smile on her face, and I knew for a fact that she was not asking me a serious question. To her, it was just a way to poke fun at the idea of someone like me being an alcoholic. I said a quick little prayer of thanks to my therapist for practicing for this exact moment before I responded with my rehearsed line.

The word "alcoholic" comes with so many strings attached. You can't use it without someone somewhere conjuring images of someone deathly deep in their addiction. Truly, asking someone in their twenties who doesn't drink if they are an alcoholic is actually seen as a joke. That is just the reality we live in. But we can develop ways of getting around those awkward—and sometimes painful—moments without betraying our own truth.

I had been scared of what people would think of me if I ever admitted to the world that I am an alcoholic. I knew the dark images that people would associate with that word because I used to do it too. So I spent the first two-and-a-half years of my sobriety meekly telling my family and friends those rehearsed lines as though I were reading from a script.

your friendly neighborhood alcoholic

Before Ian and I got married, we were living in our first apartment together. It was up the street from a corner liquor store that had everything and anything. I was there every couple of days, if not every day, picking out a new bottle of wine to enjoy with dinner or selecting that bottle of Hendrick's for a G&T night with friends.

Most days, I didn't think anything of it; this was just a part of my regular routine. But as I pulled into the parking lot one evening after work, a thought struck me. *What if the guys working behind the counter think I'm an alcoholic?*

My brother had worked at a liquor store for a little bit, and he told me about the regulars who would come into the store as often as possible to buy something to drink. They were people who were down on their luck, and a lot of them were living on the street and begging for spare change. They would gather up whatever money they could find and buy a bottle of cheap liquor. This image stuck with me, and I began to use it to depict what an alcoholic looks like. Part of it was my own naivety. Part of it was a lie I told myself so that I could avoid the truth of my own situation. A twenty-something girl with college degrees and a steady job couldn't possibly be an alcoholic, right?

That's what I had told myself for years. But that day in the liquor store parking lot, something shifted as I started to wonder whether I may have become a "regular." The mere idea of it seemed to fly in the face of what I knew an alcoholic to be, and so I began listing off reasons why someone like me could never fit that label:

I was too young.

I had three undergraduate degrees.

I held a steady job.

I paid my bills on time.

I told myself that I was nothing like the regulars my brother had told me about. I told myself that the guys who worked at this liquor store definitely did not think I was an alcoholic. And I reminded myself of people I knew who were "worse" than me. The ones who had gotten DUI's. The ones who had flunked out of school. The ones who were still living at their parent's house because they couldn't keep a job. I recognized that alcohol had become a daily presence in my life but I reasoned that I didn't fit the criteria of an alcoholic.

As I sat in my car with the engine still running, I gave myself a mini pep talk to assure myself that there was no way I could have a drinking problem. I checked my reflection in the visor mirror, laughing at myself for being so silly, and went in to buy some wine.

● ● ●

I recently saw a post on Instagram from Gentry Fawn, an outspoken figure in the sober community. It said, "Turns out healthy drinkers don't typically and repeatedly Google, 'Am I an alcoholic.'"

It was one of those posts that I just glanced at and then scrolled right past. But when the words finally registered in my brain, I started frantically swiping up to find the post. I sat there and stared at those words for a few minutes. It was like getting hit in the face with a bucket of cold water. As I look back on the years before I decided to stop drinking, I can see that I had been trying to convince myself that I wasn't an alcoholic because I was too afraid to acknowledge the signs.

All those moments when I had questioned and then rationalized my relationship with alcohol, those had been my warnings. They were small opportunities when a part of me had broken through the alcohol-fueled haze just long enough to tell me that I needed to wake the fuck up.

A healthy drinker is never in a situation where they are wondering if the guys at the liquor store think they are an alcoholic.

A healthy drinker doesn't hide the amount they drink from their partner, or their friends, or their family.

A healthy drinker doesn't Google how much alcohol is "too much" alcohol.

And a healthy drinker doesn't panic when they go to the doctor and are handed the form that always asks how many alcoholic beverages they consume in a week.

Turns out, I was not a healthy drinker.

my last

Shortly after I had decided to stop drinking, I was heading to Ohio with my dad and my littlest sister for my cousin's wedding. It was October 13, 2017. Ian was staying home because his band had been booked for a show. The plan was for me to leave on Friday night, attend the ceremony and reception on Saturday, and then head home on Sunday morning.

I had gone into the weekend with the intention of not drinking. I hadn't had any alcohol since August because I was giving the "alcohol-free" thing a try. I was committed to really focusing on my physical and mental health, and I planned to keep that up during the festivities. At first, I did great. I turned down drinks during dinner on Friday. I turned down drinks at my uncle's house before the reception on Saturday. And I started off the evening at the reception with a glass of water and a cup of coffee. At some point during the reception, though, I gave in to the anxiety and ordered my first glass of wine.

Family events have always stressed me out. It's not just the bit about being around family but what feels like the same strained conversation happening over and over and over. It is a continual stream of aunts and uncles asking how I'm doing, and whether I have a good job, and if we are going to start trying for kids. And it's the same kind of stuff with my cousins too.

I grew up in Ann Arbor while most of my dad's family lived in Cleveland. We saw them on occasion when we came into town for holidays and other special events, like graduations and confirmations, but I never really had the opportunity to get to know that side of my family because they simply weren't around regularly. There are absolutely some cousins, aunts, and uncles whom I have hit it off with whenever I am in town but it isn't the same as chatting with someone who is integrated into your daily life.

So the combination of slightly strained conversations and feeling like an outsider always gets my anxiety ramped up at family events. This time around, I thought I was doing well. I thought I was going to be able to manage my anxiety just fine. But that's the thing about addiction. Drinking was my coping mechanism. I didn't have any other methods of coping, so when the anxiety eventually got to be too much, I started drinking.

The rest of the night was not pretty. In fact, it was fucking horrible.

I drank way too much. I threw up in the bathroom at the reception. I threw up again at my uncle's house. And I passed out on the couch in his basement. My little sister (who was twelve at the time) was worried because I was, honest to God, a mess. My dad was worried too. I don't really remember the evening; it fades in and out whenever I try to think of it. But the point is that it was rough.

● ● ●

Even though I hadn't drank in a few months, a night like this was not uncommon for me. The only difference was that this time I got incredibly sick.

When I woke up the next morning feeling like I had been run over by a bus, I just did what I always did. I hopped in the shower, changed my clothes, and headed upstairs. My dad and his brother were in the kitchen drinking coffee.

I will never forget my dad's reaction that morning. There was shock and worry written across every inch of his face. I could feel his concern from across the room and it was very nearly overwhelming.

And then my dad said, "I'm surprised you're alive and standing right now."

In that moment, it all came together for me. I knew that I was done drinking alcohol—for good. I knew there would never again be a night like the one I had just had because I was simply done.

● ● ●

That interaction with my dad in my uncle's kitchen wasn't unlike others I'd had with friends after a night of drinking. But in all of those situations, I was able to laugh it off and make light of how hungover I was feeling or how little I remembered from the night before.

That morning, however, was different.

That morning, I could finally admit to myself that I did not have a healthy relationship with alcohol.

That morning, I acknowledged for the first time that I am an alcoholic.

That morning was the beginning of the rest of my life.

fomo to the extreme

Most of us live with some level of FOMO, or the fear of missing out. We compare ourselves to that friend who always seems to be on one fabulous vacation after another. We worry that we're not moving through life at the same pace as others. We feel afraid that we're not living life to the fullest, whatever *that* means. (It truly is different for everyone.) Sure, FOMO can rear its ugly head for anyone and everyone, but when you decide to get sober, that fear reaches a whole new level as you begin to notice just how much of your everyday life had involved drinking.

Why is it that so many aspects of our lives revolve around alcohol? It's so widespread that just the idea of not having alcohol can feel like a dramatic life-changing end to all our fun. I've asked myself this same question over and over again, especially in my early days of getting sober. I've even posed it to my friends and family.

How is it that something so harmful and toxic to our physical and mental health has become synonymous with fun? And why are we so certain that we can't have a good time without alcohol? I don't think there is an easy answer to any of these questions but I have come to realize that the questions themselves are flawed because, as it turns out, being sober does *not* mean that you have to miss out.

• • •

During my first year of sobriety, I was convinced that my life would no longer be fun. I was absolutely certain that I was going to miss out on all of the best things, and no one could tell me otherwise. Before I stopped drinking, my life had completely revolved around alcohol, parties, and bars. It was nearly inconceivable for me to picture a life without alcohol. In my mind, alcohol and fun were one and the same. So I fell into this negative thought pattern that confirmed my assumption that sobriety was going to be utterly and fatally boring.

The way alcohol and drinking is glamorized by society and on TV definitely didn't help, either. Every time I watched a movie where the women were casually drinking, partying, and simply living their best lives, my belief about sobriety was reinforced.

In those days, I thought sobriety meant I would have to miss out on everything I had enjoyed most. It meant losing my friends. It meant staying home alone on the couch every night. It meant I could no longer go out dancing all night, or go to a concert, or enjoy a dinner out with friends. I had believed in this warped reality for so long that when I finally did get sober I thought that even if I were to do any of those fun things, I would be absolutely miserable because I wasn't drinking.

Every time I had gone out dancing, I would drink. Each concert I went to always included alcohol. And what was dinner without a bottle of wine? All of the activities I loved doing had all revolved around drinking. I was unable to view these activities as fun, in and of themselves. Rather, I was solely focused on how I would no longer be chasing that fun buzz throughout the evening.

And on top of all that, being sober meant I would lose my identity. I would no longer be the party girl because you can't be a party girl if you don't drink, right? Then who would I be? Over the years, I had completely lost touch with who I was without alcohol. My friends, my hobbies, and my personality were all connected to drinking in one way or another.

I had conclusively tied any and every fun activity—and my identity—to alcohol. So, to me, sobriety was the loss of fun and self all at once. Would my friends abandon me when I was no longer the life of the party? Would I ever be able to go out and have fun again? As I faced down my new sober future, I began to wonder if I was destined to once again remain on the outside looking in.

● ● ●

Despite these nagging worries, I knew I was still going to start on my sober journey. Nothing could change that. But I had this extreme fear of missing out. I was continually anxious about how boring my life was about to become.

Honestly, I am so fucking proud of myself for still making the decision to be sober with all of these thoughts swirling around my mind. I opted for sobriety because I knew it was necessary; I did it despite the fact that I believed it would make me the most boring human on the planet. And I'm so glad I ended up sticking with it because, as it turned out, being sober didn't mean my life was over. It just meant I had to rethink new ways to fit my favorite things back into my life without alcohol.

when is bad bad enough?

About a year into my sobriety, I was at a restaurant with Ian when the topic of addiction came up. We were talking in hushed voices as though we were sharing some dangerous secret, and suddenly something struck me. I didn't feel like I could talk with other sober people about my history with alcohol and my journey with sobriety.

I was still holding on to the antiquated construct of what an addict was and what qualified someone to be an addict. I looked at the people in my life and those who had openly shared their story with the world. These people had it so much "worse" than me:

The friend who got a DUI in college.

The person who lost their job.

People who lost their kids and their families.

The guy who drank every night until he passed out.

The family member who has been in and out of jail.

I held each of these stories as proof that I didn't fit the bill to be an alcoholic. This was just one of the excuses I had used to convince myself that I wasn't an alcoholic while I was still drinking. And those same excuses were what I used to avoid sharing my story after I stopped drinking. In my mind, nothing "bad enough" had happened to me to truly qualify myself as an alcoholic or as someone with an unhealthy relationship with alcohol so I felt I hadn't earned the right to talk openly about my sobriety.

What I couldn't see was that my experiences *were* bad enough. They were bad enough *for me*. They were enough to clue me in to the fact that my relationship with alcohol was so incredibly unhealthy. And that's the point, isn't it? We do not all have the same story, nor do we all have the same wake-up call because what works for you won't necessarily work for me and vice versa. From where I am sitting now, I can see that, and I can appreciate it. But it took me some time to get there.

The whole story written about and around hitting rock bottom is actually so detrimental to anyone who is questioning their relationship with alcohol (or any substance, really). Your awakening, the moment when you can see that alcohol can no longer play a role in your life, is your own. It is your own story that has nothing to do with anyone else's story. As of late, I've wondered how many people have continued to slowly poison themselves with liquor because they, too, didn't believe they had it bad enough to have an actual problem.

As we chatted before our dinner arrived, I told Ian that I didn't think I could take part in any sober groups or communities. What would I say? That I had realized before something terribly tragic happened that I had a problem with alcohol? That I had managed to stop drinking on my second try?

I felt like a fraud, like my experiences didn't count because they weren't dramatic enough or extreme enough. I was convinced that no one would want to listen to my story and that no one would be able to understand. Writing this now, it seems like some fucked-up variation of imposter syndrome. I had convinced myself that I simply had not suffered enough or had it bad enough to matter.

●●●

And so, for the longest time, I kept my sobriety to myself. There were a few people who knew—mostly family and a handful of friends—but there was no way I was going to publicly announce that when I had started drinking, I didn't stop. Or that I had since made the decision to completely remove alcohol from my life.

One day, an old teammate of mine from high school had sent me the name of a woman she said I should follow on Instagram. I was surprised to see her message because, although I had posted a few casual things from sobriety accounts, I hadn't shared anything that would have overtly announced my alcoholism. But she must have seen my posts, put the pieces together, and reached out to tell me that if I don't drink, I needed to follow Sarah Ordo.

I followed Sarah and immediately listened to her sober story, and then I bought her book, *Sober as F****. I read it in one sitting; I honestly could not put it down. I finally felt seen and understood. And as I read more and more about her experiences with alcohol, my perspective began to change.

I was reading about a young woman, just like me, who had courageously decided to stop drinking. Her drinking looked different than mine. Her rock bottom looked different as well. But that's when I began to see that our stories aren't supposed to be the same. That's when I began to see that there is no one definition of addiction or of an alcoholic.

You, as a human on this planet, can determine when your relationship with alcohol (or any drug) is unhealthy and when you need to stop. Period. End of story. No one can tell you that you didn't struggle enough. There is no minimum amount of pain or suffering that you must endure. You are the only one who decides when it is time to make a change. You are the writer of your story, and you can decide when it is time for a complete transformation for the better.

• • •

When I finally realized this, I wasn't sure what to think, or do, or say. I still didn't publicly talk about my history with alcohol for quite some time after this epiphany. But this time around, it wasn't because I felt like a fraudulent alcoholic. It was because I was still putting too much weight on the opinions of all the healthy drinkers out there.

If I started to talk about sobriety, what would my boss think? What would my coworkers say? How would my classmates from middle school, high school, and college think of me? Would they think less of me if I openly admitted to and acknowledged something that I had struggled with in my life?

There was a part of me that was terrified to give up that—albeit fake—feeling of acceptance. Recovering out loud would mean stepping into myself in a way I had never done. It would mean standing up, speaking my truth, and sharing my story, and all the while knowing that I was purposefully breaking out of the status quo of drunken acceptance I had been clinging to for years.

So what's the point here? Live your fucking truth. Don't base your life choices on the opinions or expectations of others. You alone can decide when things are bad enough. Whenever you feel called to make a change is the right time for *you*. Don't live by someone else's timeline.

There will always be people out there who will judge you and your choices but those people will place judgment whether you proudly and loudly say you're sober or not. Fuck 'em. Seriously. The opinions of trolls on the internet or former classmates literally do not matter. What matters is that you made the decision to completely transform your life, and no one can take that away from you.

Your story and your voice matters. Don't be ashamed to share your story because the world will abso-fucking-lutely be a better place with it. And you never know whose life will be changed when they hear what you have to say.

the shame of it all

When do we first learn to feel shame? Why do we even feel shame? Shouldn't we be able to make mistakes and learn from them? I'll leave this one to the psychologists out there.

Early in my sobriety, shame was an ever-present—and unwanted—passenger on my journey. The first few weeks were especially terrible. I was anxious and restless as all of the things I had done while drunk continued to play on repeat in my head. We all have at least one of those memories that, when you think about it for even a moment, has your stomach in knots. That was what was happening to me. I was reliving every drunken mistake I had made—over, and over, and over again. All I could think was, *How could I have been so stupid? How did I not realize sooner that I couldn't drink responsibly?*

I felt embarrassed of my drunken stupidity. With every recollection, my cheeks burned. I kept thinking that everyone else must have known I had a problem, and that realization made me want to hide from the world. I felt so ashamed of who I was and what I had done. Eventually, I completely shut down. I retreated within myself. I stopped going out, I stopped making plans with friends, and I stopped doing so many of the things that I loved. During that time, I couldn't forgive my mistakes, so instead, I hid from them.

• • •

A few months before getting sober, I had married Ian. We had received lots of gifts from the wedding including sets of white wine glasses, red wine glasses, and champagne flutes. Plus, we still had all of the other glasses I had accumulated over the years. One evening after work, I pulled out all of the glasses and lined them up on the living room floor. Sitting on the floor, with Sharpie in hand, I wrote down each of the memories that dragged me to that place of shame. (For the record, I had enough to write on each individual glass and more.)

Ian and I then put those glasses in a box and took them over to our apartment complex's dumpster. One by one, I threw the glasses into the dumpster. As the glasses shattered against the metal bottom, I released the shame and embarrassment that had been tied to each memory. I forgave myself for the mistakes I had made. And with each throw, I could feel myself getting lighter and lighter. The baggage I had been carrying around, all the worries I was holding onto, and the disdain I was feeling toward myself finally started to dissipate. With the physical representation of those memories and that shame lifting away with each shattered glass, I was able to breathe more easily. We walked back to our apartment in a contented silence.

Don't get me wrong; there are still times when a memory will surface with a small twinge of shame and embarrassment. But in those moments, I can now conjure up the image of the dumpster, and I visualize throwing that glass against the metal bottom.

• • •

I honestly don't know if you can completely eliminate shame. It seems as though all humans are programmed with that setting for one reason or another. Or maybe it is something we learn as children, and we have a hell of a time unlearning it as adults. Nevertheless, shame can keep us from living our truth and creating a healthier future.

Shame is what kept me from allowing myself to be open and honest with the Universe.

Shame prevented me from fully healing from my past experiences.

Shame kept me from speaking openly about my sobriety, and it kept me from recovering loudly.

Shame kept me small.

Like I said, instead of forgiving myself and viewing my mistakes as opportunities to learn and grow, I had retreated. And in retreating, I continued to avoid. How can you begin to heal if you won't even acknowledge the past? You absolutely cannot.

●●●

As I approached my third year of sobriety, I started to feel restless again. It was different than before, though. This time, I had the feeling that I was supposed to be doing something more, something bigger. I just had no idea what that "something" was.

On second thought, I think I knew the entire time what I was being pushed to do. (Actually, I am certain I knew.) But I had shied away from it because I knew that the moment I acknowledged it, I would have to bare my soul to the world and I honestly wasn't ready for that yet. I was still hiding behind my shame and my fear.

Eventually, the day came when I couldn't procrastinate any longer. So I decided to share the intimate details of my story with the people of Instagram. I wrote clearly for all to read that I am an alcoholic. I proudly stated that I am strong in my sobriety. For the first time in a very long time, I allowed myself to be vulnerable. I gave myself permission to pour my heart and my struggles out on the page (or, more accurately, in the caption of my Instagram post).

After I finished posting, I threw my phone across the room like it had suddenly caught on fire. I didn't want to know if people liked it. I didn't want to read any comments. I just laid back on the carpet and closed my eyes. I had done the thing. I did it despite the fear. I did it to spite the fear. And I finally felt peace and calm wash over me.

Now that my secret was out there for the world to see, I didn't feel quite as embarrassed. I actually felt the opposite. I felt proud. I felt accomplished. I felt excited for what the future held rather than being ashamed of the mishaps of my past.

Isn't that the way it works with shame? The minute you shine a light on it, you realize that it is not quite as big or as bad as you once thought. Shame festers in the deepest and darkest corners of the spirit. And the only way to set yourself free is to look it in the eyes and show it that you are no longer scared of the truth.

An Instagram post may seem innocuous but it was just the beginning.

sobriety (n.)

According to the Oxford Learner's Dictionary, the term "sobriety" describes the state of being sober or the quality of being sensible or serious.

Urban Dictionary, on the other hand, defines sobriety as the following:

"What you suffer from lack of alcohol. Symptoms are such things as remembering where you live, walking straight, being able to have a conversation without breaking down into fits of laughter, etc...."

That's just the top definition. The second is, "the state in which everything sucks."

It's not until the fifth definition of sobriety that Urban Dictionary finally hits the mark: "A word that means whatever you want it to mean. A word that has changed meaning throughout time. A word that people use to make others feel inferior. A unicorn of words."

• • •

I was at work chatting with one of my coworkers when we were talking about true crime and she brought up her cousin who was in prison. As she was talking about him and what had landed him in prison, she mentioned that he was an addict.

Now, at that point in my life, I had been keeping my sobriety a secret for some time. Sure, I told people that I don't drink but everyone just assumed it was a casual decision I had made. Maybe people suspected, but for the most part, no one immediately jumped to the conclusion that I am an alcoholic.

I distinctly remember the tone of my coworker's voice when she said that word, "addict." I'm confident it was not a conscious change in tone, but to me, it was the loudest part of the conversation. I could hear the disdain in her voice. It was clear that she thought less of her cousin because he struggled with addiction.

This isn't a bizarre, one-off experience either. If I sat down with every single person who reads this book, I know we could collectively come up with an infinite number of experiences where people's disdain for addicts and addiction has been made abundantly clear.

Just because it commonly happens doesn't make it any less hurtful. If my coworker had known I was sober, would she have changed the way she spoke about her cousin? Maybe. But the point is that the majority of the world holds addicts in such a low regard. We are conditioned to view addicts as "less than," and we shame them into silence when they are in recovery. It is a vicious cycle that needs to be broken.

•••

Let's get back to the definitions. The reason I even typed out those definitions from Urban Dictionary was to highlight how fucked-up our society's conceptualization of sobriety really is.

Like my coworker, we as a society are conditioned to believe that addiction and sobriety are shameful, that they are bad and abnormal things. So when we talk about addiction and sobriety, it is through a dark lens that perpetuates those false assumptions. It's like an endless loop of inaccurate thinking.

And, honestly, that is the reason I kept my sobriety a secret for so long. It felt like this dirty little thing that I needed to hide from the world in order to be accepted. I was afraid of what my coworkers would think of me. I was worried that I would be passed over for promotions. I was fearful of the repercussions of telling my friends and family. So I kept it a secret.

Just like we have to rebel against the stereotypes of what it means to be an alcoholic, we must also rebel against the fucked-up definitions that have permeated society for decades.

Sobriety is not dirty. It is not bad. And it is nothing to be ashamed of.

So why are we conditioned to believe that we need to be ashamed of our sobriety?

My senior research study in college was about how the black community has used music to reclaim and redefine the word "ghetto." Then it dawned on me this past year that the ability to reclaim and redefine a word that society has deemed as bad is not limited to one particular group. I don't know why it took me so long to realize that we (read: any community of people) have the power to reshape words when those definitions have become wildly misconstrued or when they simply no longer serve our community.

During the first lockdown in 2020, I reached my boiling point. I was tired of keeping my secret, and I decided that I would no longer hide a part of myself that I knew I deserved to be proud of. I had reached a place of confidence in my sobriety where I was able to finally shake off the antiquated definitions I had been carrying around for years. And that's when I announced to the Instagram community that I was sober. From there, I began to openly discuss my sobriety with anyone and everyone.

But even in being open and honest about my sobriety, I still saw how these definitions were continuing to plague those around me. Hence, my decision to throw out the old definitions of sobriety and addiction with the intention of replacing them with my own and sharing them with the world.

•••

To me, sobriety is about transformation. It is a beautiful awakening where I have begun to actively participate in my life. It is an accomplishment of which I am incredibly proud. It is something I cherish and am grateful for each and every day. The day when I stopped drinking was the first day of the rest of my life.

Sobriety is light and peace. It is filled with hope, passion, and pure joy.

Sobriety is my superpower.

●●●

Gone are the days when we will continue to allow others to confine us within their rigid definitions. Those confines do not suit us. In fact, they only suit the people who aren't yet ready to comprehend the beauty of who we are.

Today is the day when you get to decide what sobriety means to you. Today is the day when you get to burn the old definition that has been holding you back. Today is the day when you get to redefine sobriety on your terms, for yourself.

Your sobriety is your own.

Your sober journey is a path unique to you.

And you get to decide what sobriety means to you.

my sobriety is my own

We are taught to think of addicts as dirty, low individuals who have hit a rock bottom further down than they ever thought was possible. And I believed that until maybe a year into my sobriety.

Even when I first stopped drinking, I thought I was an anomaly because I had never met another sober person who was my age. Sure, I had known people who had gone to rehab for cocaine or opiates, but in my mind, that was different. That was something that could affect young people. But alcohol? I truly believed that I was one of the few alcoholics in her twenties.

When I first started connecting with other sober women on social media, I was so relieved to finally meet other people my age who had experiences similar to mine. To an extent, it was reassuring because there were moments when I doubted my self-diagnosis of alcoholism. There were times when my ego crept in and whispered in my ear that maybe I had been too quick to eliminate alcohol from my life entirely.

I like to think of that voice—the one that tried to convince me that I had jumped to conclusions—as the voice of the addiction. It's the voice that fed me all of the lies throughout my drinking years. It's the voice that reassured me that I was far from an alcoholic when I first began to question my drinking. It's the voice that casually asked if perhaps moderation would be a better option than sobriety.

So when I began to connect with these women, I started to see a way for me to carve my own path, a way for me to make my sobriety my own. Through this community, my decision to be sober was, in a way, validated. The voices were quieted.

•••

The fact that I had believed (well into the first year of my sobriety) that alcoholism was something that only affected middle-aged people who sat around all day drinking was a part of the problem.

I had these mental pictures of what an alcoholic looked like and what a drug addict looked like, and they were not twenty-somethings who were fresh out of college. But that imagery wasn't something I had created on my own; this was information that I had absorbed from the world around me.

I drew these conclusions from the ads showing young people who were living the lives of their dreams because of the latest wine seltzer. I imagined addicts in a particular way because of how they were portrayed in TV shows and movies. I formed these beliefs because of the lack of conversations around addiction in my home, in my school, and in my life as I was growing up.

But all of that imagery left no room for me to think about sobriety in a way that would fit me.

• • •

There are also conflicting—yet no less rigid—assumptions about how one should go about getting sober. There are people who will tell you that the only way to get and stay sober is through a twelve-step program. There are others who swear sobriety is only possible through religion.

I've seen a lot of hate on the internet between people who are on different sober paths. There are those who believe AA is the only way, and some of them will even shame people who have chosen a different path. There are others who have decided that AA isn't a good fit for them. And then there are the people who made that same decision but also openly bash twelve-step programs. There is the group that restarts their "days sober" count if any amount of alcohol passes their lips. And there is the group that has accepted that slips and mistakes are a part of the journey, choosing instead to focus on the overall progress they've made.

But the reality is that your sobriety is your own.

Yes, you read that correctly. Your sobriety is your own.

Just like there is no one image of what an alcoholic or an addict looks like, there is no one path to sobriety. In fact, there are as many paths as there are sober people because each and every path is unique to that person.

That's not to say you can't borrow tips and tricks from another sober babe. In fact, I encourage you to do so. But if someone else's habits or actions don't work for you, that's okay. Embrace the things that help you and drop the things that don't.

Whether or not your sober journey looks similar to mine, I am here to support you and your sobriety. That is how the sober community should function, with an endless supply of love for those who have made the decision to transform their life.

In moments of doubt, gently bring yourself back to this one idea: your sobriety is your own. You make the rules, no one else. Your sobriety is your own.

more than just "not drinking"

I've talked with so many people about sobriety: my sobriety, their sobriety, or their desire for sobriety. And there's one thing that comes up over and over again. Being sober is about so much more than just not drinking.

● ● ●

When I first stopped drinking, I was so invested in my decision that I was ready and willing to make any sacrifice necessary to maintain my sobriety. That included cutting out a lot of my favorite activities.

I used to go to shows at bars and clubs with Ian and my friends. And at those bars, I would drink, and drink, and drink, and dance. So I stopped going.

I used to go out to dinner with friends and split bottles of wine, drinking until the point where I would have to call an Uber to drive me home. So I stopped making dinner plans.

I used to finish off a bottle (or two) of wine nearly every night at home. So I removed all wine, beer, and liquor from the apartment.

I used to have friends who I would call whenever I wanted to go out or get drunk. So I stopped calling them on the weekends.

I used to drink while snowboarding. So I took a break from the slopes during my first season sober.

When I stopped drinking, I did more than just not drink. I had made the decision to cut out alcohol from my life forever. And, as intimidating as it was to do it, that meant I also had to cut out anything that could even tempt me to begin drinking again. I changed my life, my routine, and my activities to ensure that there would never be a moment of weakness when I could give in or give up.

I'm not going to lie. It was the scariest thing I've ever done, and the hardest (at least up to this point). But I was determined to never have another moment with my dad like the one in my uncle's kitchen that October. So I changed everything.

● ● ●

I was talking to an old friend of mine the other day and she asked me how I had managed to do it. She said that she had tried to stop drinking but she always found herself back in the same place with a glass of wine in her hand. In the moment, all I could think to say was that I had made a decision and I stuck to that decision.

I kept thinking about her question for days. It was a decision, of course. But it was more than just a decision to stop drinking. It was a radical lifestyle change. It was sacrificing the things I knew could tempt me to begin drinking again. It was being brave enough to draw the proverbial line in the sand and staying motivated enough to never cross it.

• • •

Sobriety is so much more than just not drinking. It is the decision to wipe the slate clean and choose to begin again. This is the most important point that continually comes up whenever I'm chatting with people about sobriety. And it is one that I obviously implemented but I didn't realize that I had done so until recently. For me, it just happened as a part of my process. It was a natural step in my journey to choose the life I wanted to live.

In my opinion, one of the keys to sobriety is acknowledging that your decision to be sober is truly a lifestyle change, or a transformation, if you will. It is this beautiful, magical shift into a new phase of your life that no longer contains alcohol or, for the time being, the things that triggered your drinking.

• • •

I would like to say that I began to reintegrate the things that I loved—like snowboarding or nights out dancing—into my life early on in my sobriety.

But I didn't. I was too scared that they would influence me to drink again. I was also scared of trying something essentially new because I had never previously done it sober.

Somewhere between the beginning of my second year and into my third year, I began to explore my interests again. I took up disc golf. I started biking. And, if it hadn't been for COVID, I would have been on the dance floor on weekend nights.

Here's the thing: it *was* scary but I had a plan. I had a sober buddy to go with me when I went out, and I always had a method of escape, if necessary. At family gatherings, I used to default to drinking because, well, it's family, and because alcohol was the most accessible beverage. So I started bringing my own alcohol-free drinks to any family function I attended, even the annual golf outing and auction for my aunt's fundraiser.

It was like relearning how to do all of the things I loved, without alcohol. Just because you remove alcohol from your life absolutely does not mean that you must remove all the activities you once did while drinking.

Get your ass out there and give some things a try. If you're nervous or worried that you're going to slip, create a plan. Bring a sober buddy; someone who knows that you're sober. And work out an escape method so you can quickly exit without announcing loudly that you're feeling triggered to drink. (If you're comfortable with it, you can absolutely use a loud announcement as your exit plan too. Just be totally open with what you're feeling.) Whatever you do, pick something that works for you and brings you a sense of peace.

Sobriety is not simply not drinking. Sobriety gives you the magic to create a life that you are so intoxicated by that you no longer have the need to dull it or drown it in alcohol.

...and i'm sober

Sobriety isn't an all-encompassing term to describe someone. In fact, it isn't anything close to that. It is just one tiny word we can use to describe our lives.

I didn't always believe this, though. For the longest time, I truly believed that my sobriety fully defined who I was and the life I would lead. The shift I made from drinking to not drinking felt so massive, and not in the radically-transforming-my-life sort of way. It felt like I was tearing apart the fabric of my life, piece by piece. I felt disjointed, lost, out of control.

It was so difficult to imagine a world where I wasn't drinking. Partying was what I did. Drinking was a regular activity. Without it, what would I even do? Who would I be?

●●●

I held on to this feeling until pretty recently, actually. "Sober" felt like the only description for me, for my life. Sober. Sober. Sober. Sober. Fucking sober.

And it was exhausting. I spent so much time and energy confining myself to this tiny category. I was so wrapped up in this lack mindset where I could only think of the things that I couldn't do. This perspective was so limiting. It prevented me from seeing the possibilities because I could only focus on all that I had lost.

So, when I heard people introduce themselves in classes or groups, I was always in awe of the varied words they used to describe themselves.

Writer.

Artist.

Mother.

Athlete.

Musician.

And when it was my turn, the only word that would come to mind was "sober," like this one decision I had made over three years ago was the single thing that defined me.

●●●

I signed up for a writing course this past summer as a way to jump-start writing this book. Initially, I was considering writing about something completely different than my sober journey. Yet, on the first Zoom call of the course, I realized that I was still confining myself. My introduction was something along these lines: "Hi, I'm Natasha Mason and I'm from Metro Detroit. I am nearly three years sober, and I am here to work on writing my book about [insert random topic here]."

I had been avoiding writing about my sober journey yet there was this feeling, this pull, deep down inside of my soul that was leading me to this book I'm writing right now. But I had refused to see it. There was a part of me that still felt less than, like I was simply not enough to share my story. In hindsight, I know that sounds ridiculous. I had internalized the belief that I had not suffered enough, that I had not experienced enough, that I was not knowledgeable enough. Yet, at the same time, the only way I could think to describe myself was "sober." Now, of course, I can see the irony. But in the moment, I was so blind to it all.

●●●

I have seen so many sober women restrict themselves to this definition as "sober," especially once they begin to openly share their sobriety with the people around them. A lot of this has to do with the antiquated definitions of recovery and sobriety, as I talked about earlier. We have allowed society to limit what we believe to be possible because of these definitions. And, in turn, we have begun to restrict ourselves to these limiting definitions.

You are more than just sober.

I am more than just sober.

We are more than just sober.

I am a writer who is also traveling along this sober path. I am a college graduate with three bachelor's degrees who has decided to drop the booze. I am an almost-thirty-year-old who has been flourishing in sobriety for over three years. I am a sister, a daughter, and a woman who has radically transformed her life with sobriety.

And that's the point. You are who you are. You are who you want to be. All while living your best fucking sober life.

mental health outside the bottle

"Drinking to manage your anxiety is like doing dishes during a house fire."
I've never heard drinking described as a form of self-medication quite like
this before. And, honestly, it's jarring. Even now as I type these words, it
makes me feel uncomfortable because this analogy 100 percent calls me
out on my own bullshit I had perpetuated during my drinking years. I was
constantly falling into the trap of using alcohol to avoid facing the house
fires in my life. That glass of wine at the end of the night did nothing to
help me de-stress; if anything, it had the exact opposite effect.

The house fire analogy holds so much power. Doing dishes while your
house burns down around you; it is just so blatantly obvious that it is not
the right thing to do. You're focusing on something that, in the moment, is

so insignificant. It is a way to trick yourself into thinking you are helping, that you are doing something constructive. All the while, it actually does nothing for the bigger problem.

In the same way, drinking as a means to get through the day is just a way to ignore the real issue, and the damage only gets worse as the pull of alcohol becomes stronger. Addiction is the motherfucking fire. The question is, are you grabbing the extinguisher to tackle the problem or are you just doing the dishes?

• • •

Self-medicating is common. Like, really common. It can be so tempting to take what seems like the easy route and just keep running from the big questions and the scary issues. I did it. And I know so many people who did too (or still do).

Alcohol numbed me so I didn't have to feel. It slowed down my racing thoughts. It dulled the feeling of dread. And it distracted me from my dark days. Alcohol told me that I was fine, that my house wasn't on fire.

It was lying.

• • •

When I stopped drinking, all the feelings I had been suppressing, all the anxiety I had been dulling, started to rush in suddenly and swiftly. It all flooded my reality to the point where I wasn't sure how or where to even begin. I had spent years in this place of avoidance and, in doing so, I had set myself back so incredibly far.

Think of it this way: I had avoided my emotions, traumas, and anxieties for twenty-five years (my entire life). And I had used alcohol to avoid them. So, when I stopped drinking, everything I had been avoiding for literally my entire life came to the surface all at once.

It felt like a gut punch, and I'm using that description loosely because I haven't ever been punched in the stomach but I can imagine it hurts like hell. That's exactly how this felt, like I had just gotten the wind knocked out of me.

This is actually a super common part of getting sober but we don't necessarily hear it being talked about enough. For me, drinking had been my way to cope. It wasn't healthy and it wasn't really even coping. It was simply avoidance because I had not developed any other healthy coping mechanisms earlier in my life.

When I got rid of the unhealthy coping mechanism, I was left with, well, nothing. I wasn't in therapy. I wasn't taking any meds to help with my anxiety. I imagine it as though I was doing a raid in Destiny for the first time without having the appropriate light level, weapons, or even basic experience. I was just diving into it completely unprepared for the encounters that was awaiting me.

● ● ●

This all sounds doom and gloom, and I know that. But I would still do it over and over again, even knowing how difficult it was to finally begin addressing my mental health in a positive and healthy way.

Eventually, I did start working with a therapist to address my old insecurities, anxieties, and fears. Without the numbness that alcohol once provided, I gradually became more aware of how my behaviors were a reflection of my emotions. I also learned to gain more control over how I respond to situations, both negative and positive. And, in one of the greatest battles for my mental health, I finally forgave myself for my past mistakes, and I discovered how to gain wisdom and insight from those difficult moments.

Yes, going to therapy can be challenging. But I will choose therapy over alcohol every day.

Sure, taking meds for my anxiety and depression can be exhausting. But I will take those meds for the rest of my life before I ever consider picking up a bottle again.

Of course, my hardest, darkest days are still a struggle. But every time I will opt for those days over ones with a hangover.

I would rather fight like hell through my anxiety and depression, because here's the thing: I'm going to have dark days filled with dread and anxious thoughts whether I am drinking or not. But when I numb myself with alcohol, those feelings don't pass. They begin to compound upon themselves until I am pouring myself an even stronger drink. Then add on a nasty hangover the following morning, and those feelings begin to take over once again.

•••

My demons are less scary now. My depression is less crippling. My anxiety is more manageable. By stepping outside of the bottle, I have given myself a fighting chance. And there is no amount of numbness I would trade that for.

the drama of trauma

"Trauma" is a tricky word. It can immediately incite judgment, and it can instantly turn you into a victim. Sometimes we tell ourselves that our life has been free of trauma simply because we don't want to face what's really there or because we're afraid of what others might think. But the truth is, the only one who can truly acknowledge and understand your trauma is *you*. Don't give that power to anyone else.

My alcohol had me convinced that I had never experienced this "trauma" thing. In the moment, it may have been easier for me to pretend like everything was fine, that I hadn't experienced something that took a major toll on me and my mental health. Alcohol perpetuated that lie. Plus, like I think I've said a million times already, I used alcohol to avoid my feelings.

I continually told myself that trauma was something truly horrible, and I believed that someone who had it relatively together—at least from the outside looking in—couldn't have experienced trauma. This is an obviously false belief yet it is what I believed.

To be honest, I think a lot of this had to do with the way I had been raised (and I think this is something a lot of people my age can relate to). My parents were of the "brush it off and stop crying" generation. And while I know this was absolutely not their intention, I had internalized that concept and I began to write off everything I was experiencing—physically, mentally, emotionally, and spiritually—as nothing to complain about. Because complaining was weak. And weakness was bad.

I did the same thing with trauma. I told myself repeatedly that it wasn't "that bad." And anytime I did feel sad or hurt, I immediately wrote it off as me not being strong enough to handle regular life.

• • •

Let's go back to when I was just fresh out of high school and starting my first year of college nearly four hours away from my parents and the safety of home. I felt invincible. I had nothing but passion and excitement in my soul. Yet over the next few years, that young, beautiful confidence and energy were slowly chipped away as a direct result of staying in an emotionally abusive relationship.

This story began when I met a guy. I thought he was cool because he partied, smoked weed, and didn't seem to give two fucks about anything. I was young and eager, and I quickly rationalized away every single red flag. There was the freak-out he had when he heard I was hanging out with some of my guy friends. And the way he would be dismissive of me and my needs while only prioritizing himself. The fact that sex happened on his terms, and his terms alone. The purposefully hurtful comments. The constant comparisons of me to his previous girlfriends. And the pressure to always do what he wanted to do.

It didn't happen all at once. There were small signs of this behavior from the very beginning, but I was a young hopeless romantic and I had no real understanding of what love was supposed to be like. So, by the time things started to get worse, I had already gotten so good at rationalizing his poor behavior that I just kept on doing it.

• • •

I said this at the very beginning of this book, and I am saying it again: I had an unhealthy relationship with alcohol from day one. And I was desperate to numb myself to the hurt and the shame of my experiences.

So, as this "relationship" progressed, I sought out more ways to numb and to avoid the red flags I knew were there. I drank more. And I experimented with more drugs. And I began to rely on alcohol as my protective shield because, without it, I felt like I was breaking.

Looking back on it now, I can't even refer to it as a relationship. How can someone who claims to love you treat you in that way? The hard, cold truth was that it was never love, and it was never a relationship. But I didn't know that back then; not when I was in it, and not after I was out of it. I didn't know it until almost ten years later.

●●●

I was talking to my therapist about this in our last session. I explained that I had simply drowned my feelings and my pain in alcohol. I may have thought I was numbing everything with the shots at the bar. I may have thought I had healed because of the other people I had dated. But all I had done was continue to blind myself to the scars of my past. I continued to avoid the fact that I had found myself in an emotionally abusive relationship because pretending it hadn't happened felt easier in the short term.

I drank my way through college. I drank my way through the first few years of my post-grad years. I drank away the shame of that fucked-up "relationship." I drank away the hurt I still felt. And my alcohol held up the lie that it was simply a relationship that had ended badly, that it was the furthest thing from a traumatic experience.

That guy and those experiences are so far in my past now but it wasn't until I stopped drinking that I finally allowed myself to begin the healing process. And, honestly, during the first few years of my sobriety, I was so lost and so scared that all my focus went into simply protecting myself and my sobriety. But, as time went on, there were things that I simply could not avoid any longer, especially without a massive G&T in front of me.

●●●

Even now, acknowledging that person and that situation for what it was is not easy. I felt embarrassed that I had "allowed" that to happen to me. I felt ashamed of the experiences I had taken part in. And I considered hiding this from everyone because I feared the judgment from my friends and family, and from everyone else in the world.

If there's one thing that I've learned from my sobriety, it is that we are only as sick as our secrets. So, the more I hid from my past trauma, the more I delayed the healing process. And here we are.

There is nothing for me to feel embarrassed of.

There is nothing for me to be ashamed of.

And the people who will judge me for sharing this were never worth my time in the first place.

●●●

Trauma is real. And no one should ever feel like they need to downplay what they experienced or survived because someone else had it "worse." I did that for far too long, and all it did for me was increase the amount of alcohol I needed to consume on a daily basis.

That's the thing with sobriety: it is so much more than just not drinking. It is standing up to your demons, it is coming to terms with your past, and it is growing to a place that far surpasses the space you were in when you were drunk.

letter to self

I want to preface this chapter by stating that I had trouble finding the right
therapist for years, like years and years. I would find a therapist and things
would be okay for a while. I would feel like I was at least learning
something, albeit small, from our sessions. But then, after some time, I
would get bored. I would feel misunderstood. And I would ghost my
therapist. I repeated this pattern so many times, and it's not to say that
those therapists weren't good; they just weren't good for me.

This past year, shit blew up. Isolation due to a global pandemic was pretty
fucking toxic for most things: relationships, mental health...the list goes on.
So I started to look for a new therapist because I hadn't seen my previous
therapist for nearly six months after ghosting her for the last time.

Finally, I found someone who actually understood me and got what I was saying. I actually felt heard and seen. One of the first messages I sent her felt kind of rambling and disjointed. I was certain she would have no idea what I was talking about and would send something back that was truly irrelevant or off base. But she didn't. She got it. Like spot-on knew exactly what I was trying to express in my voice message. So I've stuck with her because she is fucking awesome.

Anyway, the reason I bring this up is because this therapist almost immediately saw that I was having trouble forgiving myself for my past. Specifically, I couldn't forgive myself for having been in such a toxic and abusive relationship. I blamed myself. I was embarrassed that I hadn't heeded those red flags and that I had "allowed" myself to put up with his horrible treatment for so long.

My therapist asked me to write a letter to my younger self. The girl who was just eighteen and didn't know better. The girl who was really still just a kid. The girl who had happened upon a really shitty "relationship" and didn't know what healthy love looked (or felt) like.

When I started writing this letter, I had no expectations. I was not convinced that it would make any difference because I was still so rooted in my hatred toward myself for what I had experienced. But, like I said, I fricking love and trust my therapist, so I sat myself down anyway and I began to write.

By the end of the letter, I was in tears. I felt like I had finally seen my younger self. That I had finally understood her. And, in that moment, I stopped hating her.

• • •

Dear baby Natasha,

You are absolutely going to hate that I am calling you "baby Natasha," but from where I am sitting right now, you are still a baby. You are this small, innocent, beautiful person with so much life ahead of her.

Looking back over everything you are going to experience, there is one thing that I desperately want you to know: you are worthy and deserving of everything great in life. You are enough. There will be people who will try to tell you otherwise. There will be circumstances that will make you doubt yourself. But no matter what, you are enough.

You may not be able to see it now, or for quite some time, but you are so strong. There is literally no obstacle that you will not be able to face head-on and overcome. And you are a beautifully kind soul.

Allow yourself to feel and express your emotions. I know it feels like you have to hide them from the world but I promise you that you do not. Cry when you're sad, even if it is in public. Laugh your amazing and charming laugh whenever you find something funny. And, yes, you will feel anger, and that is okay too. Lean into your feelings and embrace them. They connect you to the world around you, with the people around you. Your ability to feel your own feelings, as well as those of others around you, is a superpower.

There is one thing that I do need to get off my chest, and I am so sorry that it has taken over ten years for me to do this. I have felt so much anger, hatred, and frustration toward you for everything that you're about to go through over the next four years at college. I have blamed you for things that were 100 percent out of your control, and I have allowed those experiences to hold power over so many things that will happen in your life after graduation.

What I need you to know is that I forgive you. I forgive you for all of the mistakes and the slipups that you will have over the next few years. Because the reality is, without all of these experiences, I would not be the person I am today. You would not have become this person—this strong, beautiful, intelligent, empathetic person.

So keep living your life on your terms. Make the decisions that feel right to you in the moment. If and when things feel like they are falling apart, remember that, in time, it will pass. In time, you will not only overcome that obstacle but you will become immensely stronger because of it.

Baby Natasha, just know that you are loved, you are supported, you are safe, and you are enough.

—Natasha

gratitude for the beautifully imperfect

In that letter to my younger self, I was able to let go of the pain and shame I had been carrying for so many years. And there are still so many more things I wish I could tell my seventeen-year-old self. I wish I had the opportunity to tell myself that I am worth so much more than a drunken night. I would tell myself that I deserve more than the hangover, more than the fights and the tears, more than the shitty stream of boyfriends and dates, more than the drama. But if we're being completely honest here, I doubt my seventeen-year-old self would have listened. In fact, I am 100 percent certain I would not have listened. The glamorous facade of alcohol was just too appealing.

Three years ago, I regretted everything: every decision to drink, every drunken experience. I felt two hundred pounds heavier from all the regret

I was carrying. I spent so much of my time wondering what my life could have been like if I hadn't lost myself in alcohol. My life was clouded by the regret. I continued to live in the past, replaying those drunken decisions and mistakes until I nearly forgot about the present. What I was missing was *gratitude*.

•••

It feels so weird to admit this now, but I am grateful.

I no longer regret my drinking years, my drunken decisions, my mistakes. I no longer dwell on the "what if's." I have stopped living in the past.

Today, I am grateful for every single thing I have experienced. I am grateful for who I used to be because, without her, I would not be the person I am today.

•••

I used to hear people say this, and I thought they were full of shit. The idea that someone could be grateful for every single thing they had struggled through was beyond my realm of possibility. I could not understand how someone could feel gratitude for the good *and* the bad. It seemed so backward.

There is something poetic about it, though, isn't there? And truthfully, that is what life is: a series of moments and experiences that will shape our future selves.

We have the opportunity to either fight against our past or embrace it and accept meaning from it. When we fight against who we once were or what we once did, we are waging a war against ourselves. And I've been there, done that. I have spent so many years in conflict with myself because I thought I needed to be embarrassed of who I was and what I used to do. I thought that my past was just riddled with regret and disappointment.

When I look at myself in the mirror now, I can see how every hangover, every terrible relationship, every decision—good and bad—has created the beautifully imperfect person staring back at me. And yes, I am grateful for every single piece of it.

●●●

I am grateful for each and every lie alcohol once told me because, without those lies, I would have never discovered my truth.

I recently saw a quote on Instagram that said, "The real flex is turning pain into purpose." Give yourself a minute to let that sink in. That is the truest fucking thing. There was a point in time when I felt sorry for myself. I was sitting on my couch, wallowing in the fact that I had experienced what I had. I was comparing myself to all of the carefully curated people on social media—the ones who, from the outside looking in, appeared to be living the most perfect of lives.

I'm not sure what the wake-up call was but I do remember one day realizing that I would not be the person I am right now if I hadn't had my experiences—all of them, the good and the bad; they all served a purpose.

Getting sober showed me just how strong I am. It allowed me to see that my empathy and my ability to intuitively pick up on subtle shifts in energies are two of my biggest strengths. It gave me the opportunity to break free from so many of the limiting beliefs I had held, both consciously and subconsciously, for years.

My sobriety is my superpower. It is the first superpower that gave me the strength, the courage, and the knowledge to discover—and embrace—the rest of my superpowers.

• • •

So now when I think back on my drinking years, I still see the pain, and the sadness, and the hardship but I can view it all through the lens of growth and appreciation.

Early in my sobriety, I could only focus on the pain. I saw the world through the lens of struggle and nothing else. I was immersed in my shame over my drinking years, and I felt alone in my journey. Now, not so much.

At this point, somewhere between three and four years sober, I can be thankful for my past for the lessons it has gifted me, and I can recognize that those past experiences are just that: the past. Are there still times when I fall prey to those cringe-worthy moments while thinking back on my drinking years? Absolutely. And there are still times when I find myself glamorizing the memories of my drinking years. But now, when that happens, I can gently bring myself back to the present moment. I can see the person I have become and feel gratitude for the experiences I've had that have led me here.

• • •

I am no longer the broken girl who numbed her existence one gin and tonic at a time. But I sure am grateful for her.

fuck the rules

For years, my alcohol had prevented me from stepping into my truth. It told me that my life was only worth living if there was alcohol in it. It continually reminded me that, without alcohol, I would no longer be the fun, easygoing party girl I had worked so hard to become. These were the rules that alcohol had set for me. They were the limiting beliefs that had kept me small for so many years.

And those rules aren't just specific to drinking, either. There are so many other expectations that are aimed at dictating every aspect of our lives. That you have to look a certain way, act a certain way, like certain things. These rules were all BS ideas that had been fed to me by society and were reiterated by my drinking and my insecurities.

● ● ●

The day after my cousin's wedding back in October 2017, after seeing that look on my dad's face, I knew that something needed to change. I knew with every fiber of my being that I was about to transform my life regardless of the lies my alcohol had been feeding me over the years.

In that moment, my fears of missing out on the fun, of losing my friends, of turning into a boring granny—they didn't matter anymore. On that day, I decided that my life would be better spent as a sober, boring granny in her twenties than as a blacked-out party girl lost at the bottom of a bottle of Hendrick's.

Thinking back on that day, I am sometimes still surprised that I was strong enough to make the decision to stop drinking, that I was able to say "fuck you" to the world of parties and alcohol, that I could see that sobriety, regardless of how boring it may be, was the only path for me. I overcame the years of societal programming and the years of partying that had chipped away at my self-confidence and my self-worth. I beat the odds. I stopped drinking and I have never gone back.

It was hard. Sobriety is not a walk in the park. You may know it is the right decision but that doesn't mean you don't still experience moments of grief or sadness. But of all the decisions I have made in my life, sobriety has been the best, strongest, boldest decision I have ever made.

What I didn't realize was that sobriety was simply the first step toward the rest of my life. Newly sober me thought it was the first step toward the end. It makes me smile now because I can see how absolutely ridiculous and silly my thoughts were. In hindsight, I can see how incredibly far I have come. The life I have now, in this exact moment, is something I was never daring enough to imagine during my drinking years. Where I am—right fucking now—is on a path of my choosing. Each and every day, I am one step closer to the life of my dreams.

Gone are the days of playing it small, of confining my life to society's rigid rules, of limiting my thinking to someone else's ideals. I absolutely refuse to live my life based on other's expectations. I wake up each and every day ready to create a life that is mine and mine alone.

Transformational experiences do that to you; they begin to challenge your old limiting beliefs. Because the reality is, if I can be this fucking sober, well, then absolutely anything is possible.

• • •

This is true for anyone, not just my fellow sober babes out there. And it is time that we stop allowing our lives to be dictated by those arbitrary rules created years and years ago by old white men.

There is no specific way to look or dress.

Love comes in whatever form you want.

Honesty and vulnerability are two of the things that bond humans together.

Life is meant to be enjoyed in the way you want to enjoy it.

So, no, you do not need to work for some massive corporation that sucks your soul day in and day out.

Following your dreams is not irresponsible. In fact, it is one of the most beautiful and courageous things you can do with your life.

Spirituality does not have to mean adhering to a big-box religion.

And sexuality is a beautiful thing that is meant to be embraced and embodied.

Now is the perfect time to make the change you have been dreaming about. Quit the job that has been holding you back. Scream "FUCK IT" to the world as you start a business, launch a podcast, or write a book. Prioritize yourself, your goals, and your dreams. Decide that your life is going to be as fabulous as you want it to be. Burn the limiting beliefs that have been holding you back from your dream life.

I saw a post on Instagram today from this beautiful queen of a woman: "Earth is 4.5 billion years old, and THIS body gets eighty-sum years on that timeline, so I'm livin'."

Let's fucking live.

expecting fucking miracles

I was listening to a podcast episode, one of those episodes that you play in the background as you're unloading the dishwasher or folding laundry. I was half listening as my mind was wandering, until I snapped into the present moment when I heard the host say that we should wake up every morning trusting that the Universe has miracles in store for us every day.

At first, I shrugged it off. It seemed like such a wild and unreasonable idea. I mean, who just wakes up in the morning expecting miracles? But the more I thought about it, the more my mindset began to shift.

Have you heard of the Law of Attraction? Put simply, it is the principle that we will receive what we think about and what we feel we are worthy of. I initially thought of it this way: If you have a primarily positive mindset, and you believe in the inherent good of the world and the people around you, you will be predisposed to see the good. Conversely, if you typically feel negative about life, you will be predisposed to see the bad.

Easy enough, right?

Well, the Law of Attraction goes even deeper than that. First and foremost, the desires we have are our desires for a reason. We don't desire something just because. We desire things because they were placed in our heart by the Universe. So, when we recognize one of our desires and we trust that it will become a reality, we begin to embody the energy of someone who has already had that desire come true. And the energy that we put into the Universe is then matched by the Universe. Do you desire to land your first client? Trust that you were meant to have that client. Believe that the Universe wants you to have that client. And begin to feel the feelings of having that client.

Okay, now let's bring this back together. If the Universe matches the energy we put into the world, then if we are living in a constant state of doubt or fear, what will we receive back from the Universe? More doubt and more fear.

Enter: the idea of expecting miracles. If we wake up each and every morning trusting that the Universe has something amazing in store for us that day, we will exude an energy of confidence, trust, and positivity. If we trust that the Universe will dazzle us, we will absolutely be dazzled.

● ● ●

You may be wondering how my out-of-control drinking in my early twenties has anything to do with expecting miracles. Here's the thing: the fact that everything had aligned so perfectly that morning in my uncle's kitchen back in 2017 was absolutely a miracle.

I had tried a version of sobriety for a few months and had failed. Before my cousin's wedding, I had thought I could drink in moderation, and it turned out I most definitely could not. At that point, I knew I had an unhealthy relationship with alcohol. I knew that once I started drinking, I wouldn't stop. I had finally reached the fork in the road. I could make the decision to prioritize myself and my health or I could continue to slowly kill myself.

As I walked into my uncle's kitchen that Sunday morning, I was armed with the knowledge that I needed to be done with alcohol. Hearing my dad tell me that he was surprised to see me alive and standing was the last piece of the puzzle that needed to fall into place.

My heart was open and ready to receive. My mind was desperate for something more. And my dad was moved to say those exact words to me at that exact time. It was the perfect combination to shake my foundational beliefs and shatter the lies that alcohol had been feeding me. It was the miracle that led me to realize that my life was destined for so much more than messy nights at the bar with friends.

I began my sober journey because of this miracle.

I now know that miracles are possible.

I know that I am worthy of them.

And I know that I will experience countless more miracles throughout my life.

●●●

If you grew up anything like me, you were probably taught from a very young age that miracles are once-in-a-lifetime experiences that only happen to important people, to holy people, to people who are doing big and incredible things. I was literally conditioned to believe that I was not worthy of miracles or that I was simply unlikely to experience a miracle.

The idea that only some of us are worthy of miracles—and that most of us don't fall into that "some" category—is old. It's tired. And it needs to be erased from our minds. We, as humans living in this Universe, are deserving and worthy of miracles. In fact, the Universe wants us to experience miracle after miracle. We just need to open ourselves up to the opportunity.

●●●

I'm not going to lie. It's not always easy. There are still mornings when I wake up on the proverbial wrong side of the bed. And there are still days when my mind and my vision are clouded by the black clouds of depression. But, underneath it all, I continue to hold tightly to the belief that I am worthy of miracles, and that gets me through those dark moments.

That first miracle—the one that aligned everything so perfectly for me to drop the drink for good—was the first of many. And if the Universe can conspire to get me sober, I know without a doubt that the Universe can do infinitely amazing things for you as well. I mean, I went from drinking at least one bottle of wine (on a mellow night) to being more than three years sober. If that is possible, I know for a fact that absolutely anything is possible.

Now, it's your turn to believe it for yourself.

the transformation

The first time I discovered a sobriety group on Facebook, I was honestly pretty bummed. I had found a group that I thought would be filled with sober women who were lifting each other up, celebrating each other's big wins, and sharing their own tips from their sober journeys. The group, however, turned out to be primarily geared toward women who were trying to get sober.

I do want to clarify here. These types of groups are extremely beneficial; they provide support for women who are going through one of the most difficult transitions of their lives. If I had found a group like that in my early days of sobriety, I know for a fact that it would have been incredible.

But by the time I found these groups, I had already made the definitive decision to be sober. I was at the point in my sobriety where I was no longer contemplating trying to drink in moderation. I knew that I was done with alcohol for good. And in knowing this, I was also uncovering the desire to explore my next steps. I felt called to do something more. I felt this pull toward a much different life. At that point, I was looking for a group of women who were at this same stage in their sobriety. I just couldn't find one that felt like home.

At first, I tried to make do with the resources that were already available. I joined more Facebook groups like the one I had found initially. I dove into the personal development space. I bought all of the books, listened to all of the podcasts, and began following inspirational women on Instagram. My thinking was that I could receive sobriety support through the Facebook groups and then find inspiration to transform my life in everything else I was eagerly consuming. But there was always something missing. There was always a small bit of something that I felt was possible but I had no idea where to find it.

I continually looked at everything around me, wondering where I would uncover that elusive "something." But I was always looking outside of myself, never within. As it turned out, my moment of transformation was within me all along, just waiting to be discovered. I simply wasn't ready to see it yet.

● ● ●

You see, I do this thing where I purposefully ignore signs from the Universe the first hundred times. Sometimes I see the sign and I think there's no way that sign could be meant for me. Yup, I basically tell the Universe that she's obviously made a mistake. And then other times, I accept that the sign is intended for me but I allow fear to cloud my vision.

Fear of being vulnerable, fear of trying something new, fear of expanding into a fuller version of myself.

That's what I did here. I avoided, and denied, and blocked every single sign from the Universe until finally I wasn't able to turn away from it any longer. The way I think about this now is that the Universe was standing up, exasperatedly throwing her hands up in the air and shouting, "Alright then, Natasha. Now will you fucking listen?"

So, yeah, that exact thing happened as a part of this story. I was working my nine-to-five job and chatting with one of my friends on the company Skype when she suggested that I should host events for sober women. Then during my therapy session on my lunch break later that day, my therapist suggested the same thing. I also began seeing ads on Facebook and Instagram for alcohol-free liquor. And I got an email from this coach I follow on Instagram that literally said, "Stop second-guessing yourself and the signs you're receiving from the Universe."

If I'm being completely honest, a few other things happened that day to make me realize that this idea I had been ignoring for so long was actually the next step in my journey. Looking back now, it is definitely clear to see just how much room for growth I had—and still have—especially when it comes to trusting myself, my intuition, and the Universe.

After getting sign, after sign, after sign that one day, I decided enough was enough. I knew this was my transformational moment. So I joined a program to help entrepreneurs begin building their businesses, and I began to flush out my ideas for creating the community of sober women I knew I was ready to start building.

I envisioned a group of strong, sober (and sober curious) women who would work together to create the lives of their dreams. This community would be groundbreaking because it would encourage and support women who want to break free from the confines of what recovery traditionally looks like. It would be a space for women to write their own rules and determine what their sober journey will look like rather than adhering to someone else's program.

Finally, I had listened to the Universe. And finally, I had begun taking action to make my vision a reality.

● ● ●

I am definitely not sitting here (well, really, lying in bed) telling you that I had my massive transformational moment and now I am done. That is far from the truth. A few months after my ah-ha moment, I had a little meltdown where I (once again) second-guessed every single thing I had been working toward. All of the doubt seeped back in. For a few weeks, I even contemplated throwing out everything I had built thus far and starting over with something new, something that seemed easier to me in that moment.

Enter: imposter syndrome. I'm pretty sure this is something most (if not all) people feel at some point in their life. I mean, have you ever felt like a fraud? Or not qualified enough? That's how I was feeling during this period of self-doubt. I was coming up with all of the reasons why I shouldn't venture out on my own, why I shouldn't publish a book, why I shouldn't create this revolutionary community for sober women.

• • •

That's the thing about any transformation. There isn't really a definitive point where you have "transformed." It's an ongoing process of growth, realization, and expansion. And, during that process, there will be times when you will move in the opposite direction because we're all human and, well, fear, doubt, and self-criticism like to weigh in on everything we do.

Transformation isn't always a physical change, either. It definitely can be sometimes but I would say it's pretty rare to have an overnight physical transformation. Transformation is a shift in your mental space. It is a decision to change your thoughts and, consequently, to change your behaviors. Transformation is a state of existence where you are continually growing, learning, and expanding—and failing and trying again.

Once you enter that state of existence, it is like the blindfold has finally been removed. Or, for a better analogy, it is like Neo waking up from the Matrix for the first time. It is the beautiful realization that so much more is possible in your life. It is learning that you can co-create your life alongside the Universe. It is understanding that you get to live your life on your terms.

Sobriety was just that for me: a wake-up from the dull, monotonous world I had been living in. It was like taking a breath of fresh air for the very first time. It was a return to my truest self, and it felt so fucking great.

Every transformation from that point on has simply added to those feelings. Each time we transform, each time we allow ourselves to step into our truth and our power, we further free ourselves from the restrictive confines in which society wishes us to remain.

struggle turned to purpose

I remember seeing a post on Instagram about turning your pain into purpose. At the time I just scrolled past without really paying it much attention. It was one of those messages that made logical sense but it hadn't yet resonated with me on a deeper level.

•••

A few months later, I was sitting on my couch and journaling. I was answering the question, "What brought me here and why?" I just started writing whatever thoughts came to the surface, allowing my mind to guide the pen on the page. Then, suddenly, I felt this shift in me. I was no longer writing from that logical analytical place, and I began to pour my heart and soul into the words that were coming through me. As the words began flowing, I began sobbing. We're not talking a casual tear sliding down my cheek or even my eyes welling up with tears. This was a drop-to-my-knees, tears-streaming-down-my-face ugly cry. And as I kept writing, I kept crying. It was a beautiful release of so much pain that I had been repressing for so long. By writing those words in my journal, I was finally allowing myself to let go of the struggle and the trauma. Even after I finished journaling, I continued crying. And it felt so fucking good.

If I told this story to the people who have known me since I was a kid, they would be shocked. I grew up learning to suppress my emotions. At some point in my childhood, I had adopted the belief that my feelings were not meant to be expressed, and that any expression of emotion was simply an inconvenience and a sign of weakness. I took this belief to heart and rarely allowed myself to lean into my feelings. Rather, I pushed them further and further down, usually until they all bubbled over and manifested as anger that would be directed at whomever I happened to be around at the time. Then, as I got older, I began using alcohol and drugs to avoid and mask those emotions.

So this image of me literally kneeling on the ground, allowing all of my pain to exit my being through sobs and tears, was hard for even me to comprehend. But there I was, down on my knees on my living room floor, with both of my dogs sticking their noses in my face trying to figure out what the hell was going on.

A few days later, I saw the exact same post about turning pain into purpose. And this time, it hit me. I realized that I had a golden opportunity to make the pain and struggle from my drinking years into something so much more. I finally saw that all of my experiences—every single drunken night, hungover morning, and dark day—were mine for a specific reason. They were my experiences so that I could create something beautiful from them.

●●●

I've wondered where I would be (even, *who* I would be) if I had never had an unhealthy relationship with alcohol. I've even considered what my life would look like if I had never taken that first drink at my friend's house in high school. And, truthfully, I can't even picture it. I've tried. But I can't imagine living a life without the unique set of circumstances that have brought me to this exact point.

And that's the great lesson here, isn't it? That we can turn our pain into purpose?

We all have pain. We have all experienced trauma. We have all struggled at some point in our life. But that pain doesn't define you. That struggle, those experiences, they have all molded you into the person you are today. They have given you a unique opportunity to greatly impact the world in your own special way.

There was a point during my first year of sobriety where I was constantly throwing little pity parties for myself. I remember wondering why all of the things that had happened to me had to have happened to me. I remember getting angry and asking why it couldn't all (or at least some of it) have happened to someone else. I was angry and scared, and I couldn't see past my pain.

This is a normal response to struggle. (Yes, I did have to confirm this with my therapist.) We are absolutely allowed to feel anger in those moments.

However, anger should be just a state that we allow ourselves to feel into before releasing it because holding on to that anger will only lead to more anger. And I know this because that is absolutely what happened to me. I allowed the anger and the fear to build until I had to choose to either release it or let it fully consume me. Thank God I began to release it.

In releasing that anger, my eyes were opened to the possibilities in front of me. I began to see the different ways I could make my pain and struggle "worth it," so to speak.

That's when I began to truly share my story: the good, the bad, and the ugly. Before that point, I had still been curating the content I was sharing on social media and in my writings. I didn't want to share all of the dark pieces of my past that still kept me up at night.

The day when I truly understood what it meant to turn my pain into purpose was the day when I stepped even further into my true self. And, let me tell ya, it feels fucking great. In allowing myself to be honest, and vulnerable, and real, I know that I can be myself. Always.

• • •

Here's the thing: no one's life is perfect. Everyone has a little mess. Have you ever been scrolling on Instagram, looking at one perfect photo after the next? I have. Now, have you ever been scrolling on Instagram, seeing one raw, unedited, vulnerable post after the next? Which do you prefer to see? Chances are, the real posts are the ones that will stop you from scrolling and get you to take a closer look. When we can be honest with each other, we open the floodgates for so much connection. And that is where our truth can shine through and impact others around us.

It is an amazing feeling to be a part of a movement of sober women on social media who openly speak their truth. It is time we stop pretending that the messy parts of life don't exist. They do. And each time we share that side of ourselves, we let others know that they are not alone.

That's why I'm sharing these stories, memories, and experiences. We were not designed to go through life alone, and that extends to sobriety as well. No one has to walk their sober path solo. Each of our paths are beautifully unique but they are not isolated journeys. And that's why I share my story.

stop expecting easy

They say hindsight is twenty-twenty. I have no idea who "they" are but "they" are 100 percent correct. It is so easy to look back and see exactly where things went wrong (or how to better handle any given situation) but we can't usually access that same wisdom when we're in the middle of it. This was definitely the case for me when it came to my expectations for getting sober.

• • •

I had always expected things to be easy. School was simple for me. In fact, I really didn't start studying until my junior year of high school. And, if I'm being completely honest, that never really counted as studying; it was more like a casual review. College was the first time I truly had to put in a little bit of work for my grades.

I have also always been naturally athletic. So, when I picked a sport to play as a kid, everything just seemed to flow. Sure, there was a point in time when the only way I could continue to improve was through hard work but everything else came naturally.

The same can be said for learning a new job, picking up a new skill... There were so many things that simply came easily to me.

Now, before you throw this book across the room in annoyance, I want you to know that there is a major downside to this part of my story. Because I hadn't ever had to work especially hard, I began to believe that everything would be easy. I really did start expecting easy with every single thing I did in life. So what, right? Well, in expecting easy, any time I was faced with resistance, I just gave up.

This was the mindset I held on to for much of my life. If something wasn't immediately easy for me, I threw in the towel. Yet, the worst part is that I didn't even see it as giving up. Instead, I framed it as though I were simply moving on. I had convinced myself that if it wasn't easy, it wasn't meant for me.

Sobriety changed all of that.

• • •

I could claim that I miraculously realized that I am an alcoholic and then decided right then and there to stop drinking. But that's not true. (At this point, you know it's not.)

For almost a year leading up to my sober date, I had toyed with the idea of drinking less. There was a month when I actually did stop drinking but this was more of a reset because my tolerance had gotten so high that it took more and more alcohol to reach the level of drunkenness I was chasing. After that reset month, I tried to moderate my drinking. Then I limited my drinking to specific days of the week because I thought maybe that would show restraint.

Long story short, all of these attempts had failed to bring about the real change I knew I needed. Until that one October morning when I finally accepted that I had a problem.

Up until that point, though, I had kept making changes, thinking they would be an easy fix, and then quickly giving up because it turned out to be much more challenging than I had expected. Because, well, nothing about getting sober is easy.

● ● ●

Maybe a month after I had said, out loud to actual people, that I am an alcoholic, I saw this quote: "Stop expecting easy." And to say that it stopped me dead in my tracks would be an understatement. It's such a simple phrase. And it kinda seems self-explanatory, like something we should all just know. But seeing it spelled out on the page in front of me was life-changing.

It was then that I realized I had spent my entire life, up until that exact moment, expecting every single thing to be easy. I had grown comfortable with giving up when things got hard, when they required more than the absolute bare minimum.

"Stop expecting easy."

Those words changed my perspective for good.

There was a moment when I wondered what would have happened to my sobriety if I had never read that quote. But all that matters now is that I saw it and I fully embraced it.

●●●

Sobriety is hard as fuck. Especially during my first few years, I was challenged on a daily basis. But the old adage is so true: anything truly good is worth fighting for. Sobriety is worth fighting for.

It's time to stop expecting everything to be easy. It's time to stop giving up on yourself because you're facing a roadblock. It's time to own the fact that life will always have its challenges, and that you are more than capable of overcoming them.

owning it with pride

Hi, my name is Natasha, and I am sober as fuck.

I tell everyone now. Friends, family, coworkers...anyone and everyone. Why? Because I am proud of the fact that I am sober. I am proud of the fact that I haven't had a drop of alcohol for more than three years.

Take this as your sign that you are allowed to be proud regardless of what the world tells you.

I am proud as fuck that I am sober as fuck.

the end

I used to be ashamed of my drinking years. I used to be embarrassed to tell people I don't drink (let alone *why* I don't drink). I used to hide this big part of myself from the world because it felt dirty and wrong.

The day I decided to start sharing about my sobriety was a pivotal moment. It was the first time I bared my soul to the world, knowing that there would be backlash. But I did it anyway.

● ● ●

When I first stopped drinking, I felt alone. I felt broken, like I had somehow messed things up, and that I had brought my addiction upon myself. It fucking sucked.

I lost friends.

I was scared to do the things that I loved out of fear of falling back into my old drinking patterns.

I grew distant from my family, my friends, and Ian as I began to put up walls around myself to protect my sobriety.

I became so overwhelmed with my anxiety, depression, and OCD that I truly thought I was going crazy.

The first few years of sobriety were so challenging. I was fighting to stay sober. I was learning new coping skills to manage my mental health. I was feeling every single emotion because I no longer had alcohol to suppress them. It was a lot.

But I had some incredible and amazing people in my life who held the hope for me when I believed all hope was lost. They were my rock during this tumultuous period. They stood by me and supported me. They cheered me on, even when all they saw in return was the wall I had put up around myself.

● ● ●

Sometimes I think that I did it the hard way. AA never resonated with me, so I never went. I didn't want to open up to too many people about my sobriety, so at times, I truly felt like I was doing it all on my own.

My third year of sobriety was my life glow-up. I started to get involved in some of the hobbies and activities I had once loved (and still love). I began to branch out more, meeting new people and making new friends.

After two years of shrinking, hiding, and retreating, I was finally expanding. And, as I was expanding, I knew that my experiences and my story were no longer just mine. They were something that I was going to share with the world.

It's not easy to talk about drinking alone in my parent's basement while I was still in high school. Nor is it easy to recount all of the time I had spent searching for the next party and the next drink. Yet I am telling my story and sharing these most vulnerable parts of my past because if there is just one single person who reads this and feels less alone, it will all be worth it.

about the author

Natasha is an author and entrepreneur living with her two dogs out in the country in Michigan. Her vision is to create a space for women exploring an alcohol free life. And she has created The Sober Sister Project, a community for sober and sober curious women. She shares her story and her struggles and her mistakes in the hope that, in reading it, just one person no longer feels quite so alone.

Made in the USA
Monee, IL
04 August 2021